Qualitative Research Writing

Sara Miller McCune founded Sage Publishing in 1965 to support the dissemination of usable knowledge and educate a global community. Sage publishes more than 1000 journals and over 600 new books each year, spanning a wide range of subject areas. Our growing selection of library products includes archives, data, case studies and video. Sage remains majority owned by our founder and after her lifetime will become owned by a charitable trust that secures the company's continued independence.

Los Angeles | London | New Delhi | Singapore | Washington DC | Melbourne

Qualitative Research Writing

Credible and Trustworthy Writing from Beginning to End

Michelle Salmona
Institute for Mixed Methods Research and Adjunct Professor, University of Canberra

Dan Kaczynski
Professor Emeritus, Central Michigan University and Professor, University of Canberra

Eli Lieber
University of California, Los Angeles

QUALITATIVE RESEARCH METHODS SERIES

Series Editor: David L. Morgan, Portland State University

The *Qualitative Research Methods Series* currently consists of 63 volumes that address essential aspects of using qualitative methods across social and behavioral sciences. These widely used books provide valuable resources for a broad range of scholars, researchers, teachers, students, and community-based researchers.

The series publishes volumes that includes the following:

- Address topics of current interest to the field of qualitative research.
- Provide practical guidance and assistance with collecting and analyzing qualitative data.
- Highlight essential issues in qualitative research, including strategies to address those issues.
- Add new voices to the field of qualitative research.

A key characteristic of the Qualitative Research Methods Series is an emphasis on both a *"why"* and a *"how-to"* perspective, so that readers will understand the purposes and motivations behind a method, as well as the practical and technical aspects of using that method. These relatively short and inexpensive books rely on a cross-disciplinary approach, and they typically include examples from practice; tables, boxes, and figures; discussion questions; application activities; and further reading sources.

New volumes in the Series include:

Qualitative Research Writing: Credible and Trustworthy Writing from Beginning to End
Michelle Salmona, Dan Kaczynski, and Eli Lieber

Crafting Qualitative Research Questions
Elizabeth (Betsy) A. Baker

Narrative as Topic and Method in Social Research
Donileen R. Loseke

Introduction to Cognitive Ethnography and Systematic Field Work
G. Mark Schoepfle

Photovoice for Social Justice: Visual Representation in Action
Jean M. Breny and Shannon L. McMorrow

Hybrid Ethnography: Online, Offline, and In Between
Liz Przybylski

For information on how to submit a proposal for the Series, please contact:

- David L. Morgan, Series Editor: morgand@pdx.edu
- Helen Salmon, Publisher, Sage: helen.salmon@sagepub.com

FOR INFORMATION:

2455 Teller Road
Thousand Oaks, California 91320
Email: order@sagepub.com

1 Oliver's Yard
55 City Road
London, EC1Y 1SP
United Kingdom

Unit No. 323-333, Third Floor, F-Block
International Trade Tower
Nehru Place, New Delhi – 110 019
India

18 Cross Street #10-10/11/12
China Square Central
Singapore 048423

Copyright © 2024 by Sage.

All rights reserved. Except as permitted by U.S. copyright law, no part of this work may be reproduced or distributed in any form or by any means, or stored in a database or retrieval system, without permission in writing from the publisher.

All third-party trademarks referenced or depicted herein are included solely for the purpose of illustration and are the property of their respective owners. Reference to these trademarks in no way indicates any relationship with, or endorsement by, the trademark owner.

Printed in the United States of America

Library of Congress Control Number: 2023948298

ISBN: 978-1-0718-1810-7

This book is printed on acid-free paper.

Acquisitions Editor: Leah Fargotstein

Editorial Assistant: Jennifer Milewski

Production Editor: Vijayakumar

Copy Editor: Diane DiMura

Typesetter: TNQ Technologies

Indexer: TNQ Technologies

Cover Designer: Dally Verghese

Marketing Manager: Victoria Velasquez

MIX
Paper from responsible sources
FSC® C008955

23 24 25 26 27 10 9 8 7 6 5 4 3 2 1

BRIEF CONTENTS

Introduction		xiii
Acknowledgments		xv
About the Authors		xvii
Chapter 1	Thinking Before Writing	1
Chapter 2	Beginning the Story	15
Chapter 3	Organizing Your Writing	23
Chapter 4	Visualizing Your Writing	37
Chapter 5	Writing About Your Research Design	57
Chapter 6	Writing About Data	69
Chapter 7	Writing Up Findings	85
Chapter 8	Writing up Conclusions and Recommendations	97
Chapter 9	Sharing the Story of Your Research With Others	107
References		115
Index		123

DETAILED CONTENTS

Introduction	xiii
Acknowledgments	xv
About the Authors	xvii

Chapter 1　Thinking Before Writing　1

1.A　Thinking About Writing　1
    1.A.1　Writing as a Process　2
    1.A.2　The Researcher as Instrument　4
1.B　Writing About Thinking　5
    1.B.1　Focus Statement and Purpose Statement: A First Cut　6
    1.B.2　Qualitative Memos　7
1.C　Keep up Writing Momentum　9
    1.C.1　Switch Modes to Keep up Momentum　10
    1.C.2　Head Off Momentum-Killing Procrastination　11
1.D　The Continually Emerging Writing Process　12

Chapter 2　Beginning the Story　15

2.A　Finding Your Place in Your Research Before You Write　15
    2.A.1　Who Are You in This Research?　15
    2.A.2　Articulating the Story in Your Research　16
    2.A.3　Engaging Your Audience　17
2.B　Keeping Your Research Design Connected to Your Writing　18
    2.B.1　Building a Trail　19
    2.B.2　Knowing What to Gather and Use　19
2.C　Digital: How Far Do You Go?　20
    2.C.1　Bringing Digital Tools Into the Conversation　21
    2.C.2　How Can Digital Tools Help You Move From Thinking to Writing?　22

Chapter 3　Organizing Your Writing　23

3.A　Plan to Organize　23
3.B　Building a Road Map: Structuring Your Thinking　25

3.B.1 Creating a Frame for Your Work	25
3.B.2 Free Writing to Capture Ideas	30
3.C Saving Everything	32
3.C.1 Version Control and Saving Everything	32
3.C.2 Naming Convention	33
3.C.3 Keeping Track of References	35

Chapter 4 Visualizing Your Writing — 37

4.A Communicating Research Thinking Through Maps	38
4.A.1 What Are Research Maps?	38
4.A.2 How to Start Making a Map	39
4.A.3 Concept Maps	39
4.A.4 Literature Maps	40
4.A.5 Mind Maps	42
4.A.6 Argument Maps	43
4.A.7 Logic Models	44
4.B Using Maps to Visualize Your Writing	45
4.C An Example Using Maps	48

Chapter 5 Writing About Your Research Design — 57

5.A Presenting Research Design Through Writing	58
5.A.1 Linking to Theory	59
5.A.2 Connecting Research Focus and Research Questions	60
5.A.3 Strategies to Align Your Research Questions and Research Focus	61
5.B Building Your Research Argument	62
5.C Different Voices in Writing	65

Chapter 6 Writing About Data — 69

6.A Using Data to Build Connections	69
6.A.1 What Are Data?	70
6.A.2 Sorting and Organizing Data	71
6.A.3 Use Digital Tools to Find More Data	73
6.A.3.1 Google Forms	75
6.A.4 Use Digital Tools to Manage More Data	77
6.A.4.1 Steps to Good Data Management	78
6.B Building Strong Data: Thick Description	80

Chapter 7 Writing Up Findings   85

7.A Distilling Emergent Meanings   85
    7.A.1 Dealing With Complex Meanings   86
    7.A.2 Developing Connections During Analysis   87
    7.A.3 Showing Relationships in Your Data   89

7.B Data Analysis and Interpretation Through Writing   90

7.C A Researcher's Reflections on Writing up Findings   92

Chapter 8 Writing up Conclusions and Recommendations   97

8.A Delivering Value   97

8.B Qualitative Conclusions   98
    8.B.1 Discussing Your Work   98
    8.B.2 Composing Conclusions or Recommendations   100
    8.B.3 Referencing the Literature   102

8.C Building Credibility Using Quality Indicators   103

Chapter 9 Sharing the Story of Your Research With Others   107

9.A Revision Strategies   107

9.B Making Your Work Easy to Find and Getting Ready for Publication   108
    9.B.1 Title: How to Identify and Use Keywords   109
    9.B.2 Writing a Strong Abstract   111

9.C Reaching a Larger Audience   112

References   115

Index   123

INTRODUCTION

This book gives you strategies and ideas on how to think and write about qualitative research; the goal being to help researchers produce strong outcomes to share with their audience. Practical guidance and assistance are provided for researchers who are looking to build connections between their central research question, their research design, their analysis strategies and how their findings are presented. Researchers who are starting a new project, or in the midst of an existing project, will find this book valuable. Concrete examples are included to address key issues and provide practical steps in the writing of high-quality qualitative research.

Finding your researcher voice to tell a strong story about your research to both yourself and others is a difficult hurdle for many to cross. Having worked with doctoral candidates and faculty for over two decades, we know this book will provide valuable assistance in filling this gap for researchers. Making a sound argument, building connections and weaving your voice into your writing connects you, the researcher, to your intended audience.

Many qualitative texts dabble in what we are talking about, often in somewhat philosophical or theoretical ways. Our book focuses on applied and useful steps to assist the researcher write successfully about their research. Practical strategies designed to aid the researcher in connecting relevant content to their research are provided for a wide range of scholarly qualitative writing, such as dissertation/thesis, journal articles, evaluation reports, and policy papers.

A unique feature of this qualitative research writing book is the inclusion of the benefits of bringing digital tools into the conversation. Increasingly digital tools are being used in qualitative research and it is important to recognize how technological tools can help to strengthen writing. As such, discussions about different digital tools will be woven throughout the book.

This book takes you through the process of writing from beginning to end. Chapter 1 will help you to position yourself as a writer with upfront thinking before you start. Of particular importance in upfront thinking is the clarification of your research focus and purpose. Chapter 2 explains how to connect your research design to your writing, and brings digital tools into the conversation to help you move from thinking to writing. Chapter 3 offers ideas about organizing your writing, with tips and strategies to structure your work. Then Chapter 4 introduces strategies to visualize your writing with the use of maps, diagrams and figures. Chapter 5 discusses the use of research design in your writing and Chapter 6 moves from data management to writing about your data, and building and describing connections in your data. Chapter 7 shows how to extend your writing with the presentation and discussion of findings and dealing with complex qualitative meanings. Chapter 8 deals with writing up conclusions and recommendations. Finally, Chapter 9 is about sharing the story of your research with others.

ACKNOWLEDGMENTS

We wish to express our sincere appreciation to our partners and children who both supported and tolerated us expending energy and time on this project. In particular, Michelle would like to extend her own gratitude and love to Joe, Maddy, and Lainey.

We also thank Sara Grummert for her contribution and support with the development of this book. Finally, we must thank David Morgan, Leah Fargotstein, and Jennifer Milewski for helping us to shape both the initial draft and the final work. We couldn't have done it without them.

We would like to thank the following reviewers for their comments and suggestions on how to strengthen the book:

Aimee Adams, Lehigh University
Meera Alagaraja, University of Louisville
Meagan Call-Cummings, George Mason University
Allison Cammer, PhD, RD, University of Saskatchewan
Bryan Duckham, Southern Illinois University Edwardsville
John R. Goss III, Shenandoah University
Timothy C. Guetterman, Creighton University
Bryce Hughes, Montana State University
Deidra Faye Jackson, University of Mississippi
Stephanie J. Jones, Texas Tech University
Saili Kulkarni, San José State University
Abbey B. Levenshus, Butler University
Peiwei Li, Lesley University
Thalia Mulvihill, Ball State University
Dr. Siomonn Pulla, Royal Roads University
Michael Simonson, Nova Southeastern University
Carolyn Sipes, Walden University
Andrew N. Smith, Suffolk University
Kathryn Strom, California State University, East Bay
Kristina Taylor, Adler University
Inci Yilmazli Trout, University of the Incarnate Word

ABOUT THE AUTHORS

Michelle Salmona serves as president (co-founder) of the Institute for Mixed Methods Research (IMMR) with an academic appointment as adjunct professor at the University of Canberra, Australia. She has authored multiple books and academic papers including her book co-authored with Dan Kaczynski and Eli Lieber, *Qualitative and Mixed Methods Data Analysis Using Dedoose: A Practical Approach for Research Across the Social Sciences* (2020). Michelle has been working for over 20 years as a mentor in writing about strong research, and a teacher in qualitative data analysis and the use of Qualitative Data Analysis Software (QDAS). In addition, she is a credentialed project management professional (PMP) and senior fellow of the Higher Education Academy, United Kingdom.

Michelle is a specialist in qualitative and mixed methods research design and analysis, and works as an international consultant in program evaluation, research design, and mixed-methods and qualitative data analysis using digital tools. Her research focus is to better understand how to support doctoral success and strengthen the research process and build data-driven decision-making capacity through technological innovation. Recent research includes exploring the changing practices of qualitative research during the dissertation phase of doctoral studies, and investigating how we bring learning into the use of technology during the research process. Michelle is currently working on projects with researchers from education, information systems, business communication, leadership, and finance.

Dan Kaczynski is professor emeritus at Central Michigan University and a senior research fellow at the IMMR. He is currently an adjunct professor supervising doctoral candidates at the University of Canberra, Australia. His research interests promote technological innovations in qualitative and mixed methods data analysis in the social sciences in the United States and Australia.

Dan is a program evaluation consultant and has more than 20 years' experience conducting state, national, and international evaluations. Leadership roles include K–12 and higher education administration and research center director with extensive experience as principal investigator of more than $35 million in grant awards. His work has been shared professionally with more than 250 professional presentations nationally and internationally. He has written more than 50 published research articles and eight books and book chapters. In addition, he has supervised over 100 doctoral dissertations and professional specialist theses.

Eli Lieber is the vice-president (co-founder) at IMMR and has spent more than 20 years at the University of California, Los Angeles (UCLA) directing a qualitative and mixed methods research and consulting lab in the Center for Culture and Health. Initially trained in primarily quantitative methods, he has established himself as a pioneer in advancing thinking about and strategically implementing qualitative and mixed methods approaches in social science research. His recent work has focused on the further development, promotion, capacity building, and effective implementation of mixed methods strategies. He is particularly concerned about the practical aspects of what we do with our data—manually and using evolving technologies. His contributions here stem from his expertise and experiences in data gathering, integration, and processing and then utilizing the results in publications to maximize value for the intended target audiences.

Eli is looking forward to continuing his work with his IMMR colleagues—a truly diverse group of individuals from around the world. The pleasure of the IMMR mission is ongoing service to building methodological capacity, connecting people of like minds, engagement and communication regarding evolving mixed methods work, and bringing the deep experience of IMMR associates into the service of those employing these practices.

1 THINKING BEFORE WRITING

Get your head straight and get yourself organized before you get going writing

1.A THINKING ABOUT WRITING

Our core intent in writing this book echoes one from Harry Wolcott's (2009) classic work *Writing Up Qualitative Research*: "The moment you generate sentences that *might* appear in your completed account, you have begun writing" (p. 9). We provide specific and actionable steps which aid you, the researcher, in moving from design thinking to writing up a qualitative study. Said another way, this book assists researchers in building connections between *thinking about research design* and *writing about research*.

As a first step, we ask researchers not just to think, but to think about the ways that they think. For example, connections in qualitative research are often built inductively, in a recursive process: Researchers cycle through thinking, design, and data many times as meanings slowly emerge, accrete, and interconnect. Expect that what you may think of as a straight line from your beginning thinking to your end write-up may sometimes be more like a spiral, circling again and again through meanings, deepening your understanding each time. This book is structured like that, both linearly and recursively—as you walk a straight line through the chapters, there will be terms and ideas (author voice, focus statement, purpose statement, data) that will be cycled through multiple times, with changing angles and deepening meanings. As you will in your own research, follow the story as it emerges and trust it.

These opening chapters are offered as strategies for getting underway by thinking through your plan of attack, sorting out how you want to approach your story arc, and organizing a writer's road map. However, before even getting to research design, you must start, here in Chapter 1, with some foundational thinking. Building a sound inquiry involves upfront thinking about exactly what the study is attempting to achieve. Framing the central focus of a study begins with knowing exactly what social problem is under investigation. Part of answering these questions involves some reflection into who is asking these questions—the researcher, whose perspective is the lens through which the world of both social problem and study is understood. Dwelling in this planning stage of a study takes discipline and a willingness to push yourself to think outside the box.

How will you do that foundational thinking? By writing. As Wolcott (2009, pp. 18–19) explained, "The conventional wisdom is that writing reflects thinking. I am attracted to a stronger position: that writing is thinking. Stated more cautiously, writing is one form that thinking can take." He goes on to share his belief that "you cannot begin writing too early" (p. 20). We will only qualify that statement by suggesting a few topics with which that early writing-as-thinking process could best begin.

Given the importance of writing in expressing your early thinking, however, it is useful to think just a little about writing itself before you get started.

1.A.1 Writing as a Process

Before you even begin your qualitative research, take one step back and consider writing not as a product, but as a process. Some of the ways to support your writing process are listed in Table 1.1:

TABLE 1.1 ■ Strategies for Getting Started

Possible Strategies to Get Started Writing
Locate a good working area (free of distractions) to use for writing
Find what time of day you are most productive
Remember your brain has finite resources—keep it fueled with healthy food, power naps and relax as needed
High stress equals less work; aim for low stress for good writing
Set aside at least 30 minutes each day to write; write something every day
Remember as you start this process that what you write is not the finished product
A blank page is only blank until you write something
Try free writing about how you feel about the research
Give yourself a reward after successfully writing, say 500 words
Put things you are not sure about into footnotes that can be worked into the text later
Develop a structure/template/plan for your writing
Write your introduction and abstract last
Small steps are great; small steps are essential; small steps keep you moving forward
Things go better if you believe in your work and enjoy your writing

It also helps to prepare your mind for the academic writing process you are about to undertake. Take time to recognize that this process began long before—and will continue long after—you first thought about your topic. The writing process is built on a set of fundamental elements, described in Table 1.2, and understanding these can help you to produce strong and thoughtful work.

Having considered your writing as a process, and one with a long history, it is also useful to consider with the same care the person who is undertaking that process.

TABLE 1.2 ■ Elements in the Writing Process

Fundamental Elements in Writing	
Planning ahead	As you begin to develop your ideas, make sure that you are reading the writing of others in your field; develop ideas; draft an achievable writing timeline; develop a schedule; be flexible to accommodate changes around you; keep reading; find ways to keep on motivating yourself. Take all of this, try different things, try changing things around and find what works for you.
Brainstorming	Here you are planning, researching, gathering, and outlining ideas, and beginning to develop a working problem statement. What is your overarching topic? What do you want to say about this topic? Who is your audience? What is the "so what" factor about your reading? Why does your work matter? Gather ideas, both good and bad. Thinking and talking to others can help you to get started.
Getting ready	At this point, you are looking to better understand your topic and find authoritative sources to make your writing stronger. Then you create the outline for your story which will help you to map out and organize your ideas so that your writing will flow for the reader. Remember it is your job to help the reader navigate through your work and your thinking.
Building content	This is the time to start creating sentences and paragraphs to make your arguments. This draft does not need to be perfect but here you want to write your ideas in a way that's organized with strong transitions between sentences and paragraphs. Read your work aloud, either as you go or after you have finished, to help you hear gaps in information, and any awkward transitions.
Fine tuning	Here you are looking for a natural flow in your story and a chance to fine tune your writing. Does your draft writing give the reader a complete picture? Also take this time to simplify and clarify your writing by removing unnecessary words and making your writing more concise.

(Continued)

TABLE 1.2 ■ Elements in the Writing Process *(Continued)*	
Fundamental Elements in Writing	
Almost finished	This is where you are almost finished with your writing and focusing on proofreading for technical issues like spelling and grammar. Rereading your work at this point can be quite difficult as you have become very close to your work over the time you have spent producing it. Clear your mind and give it a complete last critical read (line by line might help)—see if you have built the connections needed for your reader to follow your story.

1.A.2 The Researcher as Instrument

As the writer, you are guiding the reader through the research design of your study from start to finish. In so doing, you are not only sharing the story of your research design and results, but you are also sharing your unique perspective on this story. Qualitative writing involves a reflective openness in sharing your perspective and voice: Who you are and what you bring to the inquiry are essential elements which help enrich qualitative research. In this sense, you are the researcher as instrument, critically examining your potential impact upon the naturalistic setting as well as the entire research process (Patton, 2015, p. 70; Schwandt, 2015, p. 268). You, the researcher, drive the inquiry including parsing the world into a particular order, focusing on a finite area within that order, identifying a problem area, articulating research questions, designing research methods, conducting analysis, developing findings, and interpreting meanings.

Knowing who you are as a researcher regarding any particular study is an important element of the study design. This first chapter is intended to challenge you to consider critically a key question. What, and where, is your voice in this inquiry? Finding and knowing your voice is essential to telling the story of your study. Having a better understanding of how your voice as a writer can be shaped by who you are as a person is part of this. For example, who you are as a writer can be fundamentally defined by the following:

- Who you are as a person in your academic field
- What your role is as a student, working professional, or a social science researcher
- How you are located in and shaped by your community and larger society

- How you position yourself with the people and phenomena you are observing
- How you position yourself in the research story you are telling

The very nature of social science research involves the study of society and social relationships. As a qualitative researcher, your inquiry into such human interactions places you into the role of shaping and defining the path of inquiry. This role raises numerous philosophical and theoretical tensions which must be carefully considered throughout your study. The questions above may be answered in a number of different ways—but they must be answered. In the end, you must share your purpose and role of researcher in a clear and articulate manner and show how this approach is a strength rather than a limitation. The chapters to come will circle back numerous times to this question of voice, so you do not need to end this inquiry now—you just need to begin it and to continue to be aware of it.

Having addressed yourself to writing in numerous ways, you are now ready to begin the kind of writing that will help you discern what you think.

1.B WRITING ABOUT THINKING

As you start to think about your research, your initial writing begins with you deciding where to begin your story. It is your job to outline your thinking for the reader. This can be done by thinking about your qualitative research writing as addressing a social issue by considering the following:

- Introducing the reader to the problem being considered
- Informing and updating the reader with relevant background research
- Presenting your methodological plan
- Discussing your findings
- Presenting recommendations you have drawn from your work

In this process, you start with your social issue—or more specifically, with beginning to articulate where you as a researcher intersect with the issue that interests you. Not only do you have a focus in addressing this issue, you also have a purpose.

1.B.1 Focus Statement and Purpose Statement: A First Cut

You may find it somewhat unsettling to accept the point that the driving purpose of your qualitative study arises from you, the research instrument. Given this charge, your writing must provide the reader with a clear and articulate message about your agenda. What brought you to this issue? What are the connections and reasons behind your interest in studying this topic and what do you intend to achieve?

As you are developing your thinking, it is essential to formulate and craft the focus statement for your research, which is then elaborated by writing a purpose statement. This pair of foundational statements will serve as constant touchstones, frameworks and guides from articulating your research design all the way through to writing up your results.

A focus statement is a carefully crafted sentence that expresses what your study is about and defines the parameters of your qualitative argument. Again, as with voice, later chapters will cycle back through the creation of focus and purpose statements, deepening them each time. For more about focus statements refer to Section 5.A.2, Connecting Research Focus and Research Questions, and Section 5.B, Building Your Research Argument. A purpose statement then alerts the reader to the direction your paper will take through that qualitative argument, with reference to methodology and research design. A qualitative purpose statement is not an explanation of what you intend to prove or disprove. Rather, it must be an open and reflexive explanation of your connections to the topic and social problem under consideration. For an example of a focus and purpose statement, please see Section 4.C.

At this point in your writing, though, consider who you are, and what is your own voice in the research. As you develop your writing, ask yourself about your research purpose: For example, is this a critical theory study intended to critique and liberate, or is this a program evaluation intended to explore and improve a specific service? How can you strengthen your style of writing to be more appropriate for the intended purpose of your study? What steps might you take to share your research agenda and strengthen your voice in your study for your audience?

A purpose statement may be written as a preamble to a section that presents the study's focus statement and key research questions. Another approach is to separate this discussion of your research purpose into a particular section that covers a broader discussion addressing your role as researcher. Regardless of the approach you take, this discussion must be developed sufficiently so that your audience has a clear understanding regarding your connections to the topic and to the social importance of the study.

This book is not intended as a qualitative research methods textbook. It is a textbook about getting underway and moving forward with your writing as your progress through the qualitative process of inquiry. Suggested readings are highlighted throughout this book providing more detailed discussions into qualitative research practices. As an example of more detailed readings, the following selections are provided to specifically assist in your exploration into *writing your focus and purpose*:

Brodsky, A. E. (2008). In L. M. Given (Ed.), *The SAGE encyclopedia of qualitative research methods* (Vol. 2). SAGE. **[Researcher as Instrument, pp. 766–767]**

Salmona, M., Lieber, E., & Kaczynski, D. (2020). *Qualitative and mixed methods data analysis using Dedoose*. SAGE. **[Framing the Purpose and Focus, pp. 16–18]**

Patton, M. Q. (2015). *Qualitative research & evaluation methods* (4th ed.). SAGE. **[Clarity About Purpose, pp. 248–250 & Empathic Neutrality, pp. 58–62]**

1.B.2 Qualitative Memos

Taking the next step in your process of writing-as-thinking can be facilitated using memos. Qualitative memos share similarities with other forms of documenting research development such as diaries, journals, audio/video recordings, or blogs. The use of memos, however, stands apart from these other forms of documentation and is increasingly recognized in the research literature as an important step in qualitative inquiry. You are the qualitative researcher who is driving the inquiry. As such, you need a place for tracking your emergent thinking especially because as "the project grows . . . your ideas become more complex and, later more confident" (Richards, 2015, p. 92). Maxwell (2013) uses memos as a tool to stimulate thinking as well as a writing strategy for making early drafts. He offers the following insights into the importance of memo writing:

> [Memos] are ways of getting ideas down on paper (or a computer), and of using this writing as a way to facilitate reflection and analytic thinking. When your thoughts are recorded in memos, you can code and file them just as you do your field notes and interview transcripts, and return to them to develop the ideas further. Not writing memos is the research equivalent of having Alzheimer's disease; you may not remember your important insights when you need them. (p. 20)

For the purposes of this discussion, we put forward four types of memos (refer also to Table 1.3):

TABLE 1.3 ■ Different Types of Memos

Different Types of Memos	
Methods	• Describes the basis for design decisions • Provides a trail of design changes
Reflective	• Captures your developing thinking through critical contemplation • Self-monitors researcher as instrument
Analytic	• Explains preliminary understandings • Illuminates the researcher's interpretive processes
Inductive–Deductive Shifts	• Captures intentional/unintentional shifts in thinking • Notes differences between qualitative/quantitative reasoning

1. Methods memos provide a helpful means of capturing developments and changes in the research plan which often unfold in qualitative studies. A well-documented flexible emergent design is considered an essential strength when conducting qualitative inquiry.

2. Reflective memos are useful in capturing your role as researcher-as-instrument. Before a research study appears in written form, there is considerable prior work. The researcher has given the research topic considerable thought and discussion with others. This journey of thinking and talking needs to be captured in written form. Capturing developments in your evolving role as researcher provides a means to document this journey of inquiry. A collection of reflective memos will also prove useful when you write or refine your purpose statement for the study.

3. Analytic memos can explore and express many theoretical orientations and are key to the tracking of design and analytical thinking and development during any research project (Charmaz, 2014; Corbin & Strauss, 2015; Patton, 2015; Saldana, 2013; Salmona, Lieber & Kaczynski, 2020).

4. Inductive–Deductive Shifts memos may also be adopted in a study where the researcher is exploring the unique challenges they may be experiencing as they view and interpret data. Knowing when and how you are interpreting qualitative meanings enhances your

awareness and improves your ability to articulate clearly how you are functioning as researcher-as-instrument.

The suggested length of a memo is usually one to three paragraphs to be most useful—shorter and you may not be able to adequately capture your thoughts; longer and you will find that you are likely memoing about multiple thoughts and ideas which are better described separately. You may find that short notes made during discussions, such as annotations, notes-to-self, or observer comments, may be expanded upon in greater detail through a memo. Short notes are useful bookmarks but are not a substitute for writing a memo. Conversely, when the length of a memo begins to grow you need to consider where one topic ends and another begins. In such a situation, break the memo apart into additional memos covering different topics.

As you write your memos, you are creating a documented trail of your developing researcher insights and decisions. This is particularly critical as your study progresses and becomes increasingly complex. As well as using your memos as a record of your research and data, you can also use your memos to recreate your thinking, and path taken through your inquiry, when you come to write up your research. Further, memos promote your ability to better communicate with your stakeholders over the course of a research project.

Of particular importance to this discussion is the value of using any number or type of memos as credible qualitative data. Because qualitative data represent items of social meaning, a memo discussing qualitative data and inductively building meaning *itself comprises a qualitative data point*. Later chapters discuss qualitative data and the ways that memos both interpret and comprise data; the point here is that writing memos creates multiple layers of value for a qualitative researcher.

A helpful rule to follow about memos is to *write early* and *write often*.

> Regardless of the number of memos you write, you will always think later that you could have written more.

1.C KEEP UP WRITING MOMENTUM

Now you have started writing, how do you keep your momentum? Memos are a great way to start writing; however, just as starting can be hard, keeping going can also be challenging. How do you stop yourself getting caught in the detail? At this point you need to be looking at the bigger picture and how things fit together. See Table 1.4 for some ideas and strategies for keeping your momentum.

TABLE 1.4 ■ Strategies for Keeping Going

Strategies as Your Writing Builds

Start slowly and build	Developing any line of argument to weave through your story is always tricky and challenging. Take small steps at first and build a strong foundation for your story arc.
Start somewhere	Sometimes you don't know where to start. Don't worry it is ok to start anywhere. The beginning of your book is critical, but most writers don't write the beginning until the end anyway. Often you don't know how to start until you get to the end. So, get going, start anywhere.
Guide your audience	It is your job to help the reader navigate your work and there are lots of techniques that can help you with this. Signposting (preparing the reader for a change in the direction of your argument), topic sentences (showing the relationship of the paragraph to your central argument and outlining what to expect in the following paragraph), and the given-before-new principle (where the writer expresses known information before any previously unknown related information in their writing). These techniques are neither the first thing a writer needs to address, nor are they the last. They are proven strategies to help you present an argument with a logical flow that gives guidance to the reader.
Synopsis—Outline your story	Find a way to work out your story arc. If this doesn't make sense to you, it will never make sense to the reader. Addressing your central problem with the structure of an outline or with a synopsis can really help you to tell a strong story.
Just write!	Be gentle with yourself and allow yourself to write badly. Get something on to the paper, and later you can rewrite and polish your work. Much easier to work on something rather than nothing.

1.C.1 Switch Modes to Keep up Momentum

Everyone works in different ways and has days where they are unable to crystallize their thinking and write. On such days it is still possible to move forward with your work by switching modes among thinking, talking and writing.

These three ways to handle ideas take place at different speeds. Generally, "just thinking" is the fastest, talking is slower than thinking, and writing is even slower than thinking and talking. Note that talking can serve as a bridge between the fast-flowing "just thinking" and the much slower stage of writing. When talking about your ideas you are verbally sharing your idea with others. You may find it helpful to make an audio recording as you verbalize your thinking. The recording can be used later when you transfer your thinking to writing. Effective verbal communication demands that you structure your message in a way that can be understood, yet retains flexibility, because if the listener is confused you can quickly amend and clarify the verbal message. Talking also provides you the opportunity to listen, gain feedback, and further refine your message.

Critically assess how you go about thinking, talking and finally writing about your research. You may find it helpful to consider the differences in your message as you shift between these three different speeds to express your research thinking. For example, you can start by developing a train of thought around an issue, then talk about it with others as you refine your thinking, and then finally craft it in writing.

1.C.2 Head Off Momentum-Killing Procrastination

As you consider how you organize yourself to write successfully, remember that distractions abound and can easily cause you to stray from getting going with your writing. No doubt you are well aware of some of your behaviors and habits that interfere with sitting down and getting on with it. Knowing this, take the time now to find ways to minimize and overcome distractions and blocks. Can you identify what may be stopping you writing? Take a look at Figure 1.1 and see if you can identify any of these daily distractions that may be blocking you from spending time writing and developing your writing routine.

FIGURE 1.1 ■ Procrastination Opportunities

iStock.com/fleaz, jamtoons, Kittisak_Taramas, primiaou, youhhou

Plan now how you intend to change your behavior to avoid or deal with these distractions. It is important that you establish a productive routine and stick with it.

> A tip for achieving a productive routine: Always keep forward momentum by setting yourself achievable goals. For example: Today I will write a paragraph on . . .

1.D THE CONTINUALLY EMERGING WRITING PROCESS

As your early writing begins to accumulate, your thinking will become more accessible to you. Connections and relationships will suggest themselves and an early framework will begin to emerge. You will write your way to more coherent meanings. Revision is part of this process. Badley (2020) outlines a number of important considerations about how academic writing can lead to ways of continuously learning to improve. As you revise and edit drafts of your work you will increasingly see improvements at each stage.

Now you have a routine (or are thinking about a routine) and are beginning to write. Take some time to think about writing skills and which areas will benefit from improvements. Table 1.5 (discussed again in Chapter 8) is drawn from the work of Ondrusek (2012, p. 179) who reviewed the literature and identified 12 core competencies which are considered essential for advanced writing skills.

This list presents key competencies in three main groups: mechanics and grammar (1–5); design thinking (6–7); and credibility and quality (8–12). You might find it helpful to think about your writing using these three groups when reviewing your work.

> Start with mechanics and grammar as you develop your design thinking and move through to quality.

Break down each piece of your writing and review; consider where your strengths and weaknesses lie; and find out where you can find help to improve any deficiencies in your writing. It is interesting when reviewing this listing of writing abilities that although mechanics and grammar are important, the top three essential skills involve building a convincing argument with a clear voice.

In this stage of emergent thinking, you may notice yourself reaching for structure with which to further connect your thoughts. To minimize confusion, you may find it helpful to start with an advance organizer which allows

TABLE 1.5 ■ Core Competencies for Advanced Writing Skills

Core Competencies for Advanced Writing Skills	
1	organization
2	argument/evidence/logic
3	audience/voice
4	content
5	mechanics/grammar
6	conceptualization/developing ideas/prewriting
7	process
8	accuracy
9	scholarly identity
10	sources
11	expression
12	critique

Source: Adapted from Ondrusek (2012, p. 179).

you to introduce the context of your message to your intended reading audience. An advance organizer may be an analogy, a graphic figure such as a concept map (see Section 4.A.3), or a shared understanding that you offer to the reader as you progress your story about your work. It clarifies the presentation of the story in a way that makes it easy for the reader to make connections from the known to the unknown. For example, you may first direct the reader's attention to what is important in the upcoming text, then you highlight the relationships among the ideas presented, and finally you remind the reader of relevant new information that they have already encountered. Building and organizing these connections is an effective means of making it easier for your audience to follow how your thinking is developing.

As you are writing, you will continually make new drafts to improve your work. Try simplifying your language and being clear about what you are trying to say. Complicated sentences are difficult for the reader to follow. If a sentence appears long and/or complicated, it might be that you are trying to include too many ideas. So, go back to basics and make sure that only one idea is in each sentence. Be prepared to take some of your work out of the story arc if it doesn't fit. Pruning your written work can be difficult especially when you have invested

TABLE 1.6 ■ Helping You to Start Writing

General Questions to Help You Get Started Writing

Explore	Explore the problem you are investigating, not the topic.	Identify your audience. Who will be reading your work? What is the purpose of your writing? How can you achieve this purpose? Where are you in this writing? Make a plan for your writing
Generate	Generate ideas through brainstorming.	Keep writing Be gentle with yourself as you write Try not to censor your writing at this point Always keep returning to the problem Think about your reader. What do they need to know? What questions might they ask? Will all your readers be the same?
Question	Keep asking yourself questions.	How? So what? Why does this work matter? Who? What? Where? When? Why? Define important terms and ideas What is the meaning or nature of the issue? Explore relationships and connections in your writing

Source: Adapted from Purdue Online Writing Lab (2021, prewriting section).

considerable time and energy into a particular section. Remember to keep all discarded material somewhere safe, as you may need to go back to it later.

Always push yourself to do more and challenge yourself. Remember you are trying to communicate your knowledge to your audience, so concentrate on that. Don't try and impress your audience with complicated writing and strive to keep connecting relevant content to your research.

The following Table 1.6 describes some general questions that you will revisit as your writing develops. Keep questioning, keep writing, keep talking, keep thinking and keep going.

Chapter 1 started you doing some foundational thinking about the writing process, as well as about who you are as a research writer and what you can bring to your writing. This is intended to help you structure your thinking through writing, beginning with your focus and purpose statements and with capturing your developing thinking through memos. The next chapter builds on this by helping you to further develop your place in your research and engage your audience. It also gives pointers about keeping your research design connected to your writing and brings digital tools into the conversation.

2 BEGINNING THE STORY

Now that you are underway with a starting point in your writing, the importance of positioning yourself in the study needs further consideration. In this chapter, several activities are offered to assist you in clearly expressing your intentions as a qualitative researcher. Writing offers you a platform to position you, the social science researcher, as a central voice advocating for the quality of your work.

2.A FINDING YOUR PLACE IN YOUR RESEARCH BEFORE YOU WRITE

In the recursive process of qualitative research writing, it is now time to circle back to the perspective of researcher-as-instrument as you begin to inquire more deeply into how you are driving this story of your research. Everyone has something useful and interesting to say which draws upon the sum of their own experiences. Related to this, everyone sees the world from their own point of view. A researcher's role is to be clear about who they are and what they bring to any study. Your challenge as a writer is to find out who you are, where you come from and how best to share this voice. Always be genuine and be clear how your values and world view frames your writing.

2.A.1 Who Are You in This Research?

To write well about your research you must understand who you are, what you know, and what you bring to your research. Think about how your own values and view of the world may affect how you write, and what you have to say in your work. Take time to consider thoughtfully where you have come from, who you are both personally and professionally, and the unique views you bring to the world as you see it. These insights will shape how you conduct qualitative research. By thinking about, and answering these questions, you will be better positioned to thoughtfully express your written research message. Writing can help you with this as through writing you can find your voice. Use the following to get you started on this path relating to your research:

- What relevant scholarly or professional work have I done?
- Which of my own life experiences might be relevant?
- How can this research strengthen my professional or academic agenda?

There are many ways to communicate your story in your work. High quality writing requires you to demonstrate your ability to articulate knowledge and experience. You will need to sound reasonable, thoughtful, and confident. In other words, you need to find your academic voice. You need to structure and argue your ideas and opinions based on evidence; and present yourself either as objective or as reflective about, and responsible for, your own subjectivity. Your voice will reveal your thought process to your reader. Remember that you must write with clarity and an active voice that avoids jargon. Convoluted sentences and stilted language will only confuse your reader. Strive for an authentic voice which your readers will accept as credible and trustworthy.

2.A.2 Articulating the Story in Your Research

To communicate clearly with your reader, you must create a core message which is the story arc for your research. Considering a story arc and the signposts that show the reader the way through the general structure of any story as a whole is brought to the forefront. Even though you might dig into the details when sketching an outline for your story, the story arc is a way to look at the whole from a distance. Find a way to connect and share this passion with your audience.

A really important point is that every story needs a great beginning, with clear structure and a strong ending. You won't know, or be able to tell, your story until you have finished your research. For now, you can start writing and capturing your thinking as it develops along the way (see Section 3.C.1 for ideas about version control and keeping all the work safely you create along the way). When you know the end of your story, you can go back to the beginning and design a great start that foreshadows the ending. Remember that it is your job to excite the reader and show the audience how they will benefit from reading your research. Everyone's time is important—how will reading your work help, or excite, the reader?

> Becoming conversant with academic writer blogs can help the new writer stay connected to their reader audience. There are many writer blogs for you to discover; the following two are popular sites for you to consider:
> - Chronicle of Higher Education blogs
> - Inside Higher Ed—GradHacker

A related issue to placing yourself into a qualitative story arc is deciding how and where to place yourself in the narrative. Qualitative research writers commonly ask if it is acceptable to use a first-person singular style when representing the writer's voice. Although once forbidden, the use of "I" has become more acceptable in academic writing (Kamler & Thomson, 2006, p. 59). This growing acceptance is particularly evident in qualitative writing as the researcher, through their voice, drives the inquiry. Consider your position in the narrative as you decide on your usage of "I" in your work. Researchers with a more empirical emphasis may choose to limit usage primarily to describing the purpose of their study and their role as the researcher. Researchers using their own subjectivity as part of their critical lens may choose to use first person singular throughout their work. That said, overuse may distract from the flow of story arc.

2.A.3 Engaging Your Audience

Identifying the audience for your work is crucial to communicating persuasively. When you know your audience, you can tailor your content, tone, style, and language and make constructive decisions about what to include, how to organize your work and how best to support your line of argument.

For any good writing, you must be very clear about your main idea, as the main objective of your writing is to persuade your audience to accept this idea. To begin, consider who is most likely to be interested in your research. Next, try to better understand your audience by considering if your readers are undecided about your main idea; or how your writing may be linked to a trending topic in your field. Make sure to clearly frame the social problem you are investigating and identify the boundaries of the problem from within your topic of interest. Make an effort to explain to your audience what the problem is and the value of investigating this social problem in context.

To build interest for your audience, make sure that you know which aspects of your work might attract their attention. Consider how you can promote the strongest supporting points for persuading your audience. Make sure that you present a balanced argument and carefully consider any significant opposing views in your field. When you explain a counterargument in your writing and then refute this opposing view, you will strengthen the credibility of your work. Always keep in mind how your writing will serve your audience and how your readers might react when reading your work. Also consider what sort of evidence your audience will expect that may best convince them that your work is valuable and credible. Review Table 2.1 for ideas about identifying and describing your audience.

One of the most important things about writing is to be clear about the "so what" factor. What is important about your research and why will the reader care enough to read it? Once you are clear about this, you will have a better idea who your audience is and can write something that people will want to read.

2.B KEEPING YOUR RESEARCH DESIGN CONNECTED TO YOUR WRITING

Your research design will guide the writing of your work. This includes identifying your research approach, research questions, and methods of collecting data. When you are telling the story of your research, your reader will want to

TABLE 2.1 ■ Strategies for Identifying and Describing Your Audience

Identifying Your Audience
Be clear about your central idea as the main purpose of your writing is to persuade your audience to accept this idea.
Who is most likely to be interested in your research?
Understand your audience for instance, are your readers undecided about your main idea? Can your writing be linked to a trending topic in your field?
Clearly frame the social problem. Identify the boundaries of the problem from within your topic of interest. Explain to your audience what the problem is and the value and benefits of investigating.
What is it about your work that might interest the audience?
What are the strongest supporting points for persuading your audience?
Are there any significant opposing views in your field? Explaining this counterargument in your writing and refuting this opposing view will strengthen the credibility of your work.
How will your writing serve this audience?
How might the audience react to your writing?
What sort of evidence will your audience expect to convince them?

make sure that your research design is robust and trustworthy. One of the ways you can strengthen your writing is to make connections in your story between your research focus, your research questions, and your data collection methods. To do this, make sure to keep track of your thinking and how it develops. What you are aiming for is a transparent description of the steps you take in your research from start to finish. Maintain records of every step you take in your research investigation using memos, diagrams, or spreadsheets.

2.B.1 Building a Trail

Creating, and documenting, a trail through your work allows you to track and build upon developments in your research. As you go through your research, from design to analysis to writing up, you will come to decision points. It is very important that you capture these decisions and the paths taken, so that you can revisit and review as you continue on your research journey.

> Consider creating an electronic record of your journey through your research that will do a number of things:
>
> - Catalog events chronologically.
> - Keep track of ongoing descriptions of your research procedures.
> - Provide an historical record of your thinking throughout the research.
> - Maintain a log of communications with others (e.g., colleagues, team members, participants, research supervisors).

Keeping a record of this trail throughout your work will help you backtrack to the origin of your thinking as you go through the writing process. This will be particularly useful when writing up your analysis, and a trail of your data analysis path will make it much easier to report and explain your actions. It will help you keep track of all the things you do, and change, throughout the process. Make sure you collect all useful and necessary information, and that all this work is protected and stored safely in a secure location. Also, regularly back up your work multiple times in different locations to ensure reliable redundancy in your backups.

2.B.2 Knowing What to Gather and Use

New writers are often overwhelmed trying to determine what information to gather and use. What if I fail to document something important? How will I know what will be important? How will I know if I have gathered enough detail? Not to worry—just keep in mind that you are embarking on a journey and will want to tell that story, as richly as possible, as your research inquiry evolves. As the final project becomes clearer to you, you will find improved clarity in your message.

As you work through your project, remember to always keep your research goals, research questions and research focus at the front of your mind. This will help you when thinking about how to document, your actions and thinking, as you move through the process. How is your thinking changing over time? What decisions are you making about what will be included or excluded from your story? At each of these moments, are you recording sufficient information to communicate a clear story line? How are things unfolding and becoming clearer? Remember to capture details as you write. When in doubt, look at your study focus statement. Keeping track of changes in your research design is very important, and it is always better to have too much recorded documentation rather than too little.

Your job as a good writer is to uncover the chronology to your story, and the nature of how you capture this detail will be specific to each project. Take some time to consider what will help you keep the story clear. One of the best pieces of advice one of the authors of this book received from their doctoral supervisor was, "Tell it to me like you are speaking to your grandmother, or one of your parents". Remember, they are unlikely to have much experience around the nature of your project and your research methods. How would you break things down and what details would you include so your grandmother or parents can better understand your work, think it is interesting, and, of course, be proud to see how brilliant you are becoming?

2.C DIGITAL: HOW FAR DO YOU GO?

This is an important topic for any writer to think about. How far do you go along the digital path? Are you a traditionalist? Do you like writing with pen and paper? Do you like to be organized using electronic means? How do you manage your schedule? How do you like to communicate about your research? There are no right or wrong answers here; this is just part of better understanding who you are and what you bring to the research process. What is important here is recognizing that digital tools are just that, tools to help you improve your research and your writing. Knowing what you expect from a given tool is an important part of staying in charge and managing what you hope to achieve from your work.

Using digital tools throughout a qualitative study can support the research process by saving time and adding depth and robustness to qualitative research. Digital tools can assist in collaborating with other researchers and stakeholders, managing time and the research process, data gathering, data management, data analysis, and representing and sharing your findings. In addition, an ongoing integration of digital tools for your data management and analysis can allow you to draw more widely from the data that you will work with in your study (see Section 6.A.3 for more on this).

2.C.1 Bringing Digital Tools Into the Conversation

Digital tools can be helpful to use throughout the research process to help you capture details for your later review. Any digital tools you may choose to use will not take the place of other activities that you will engage in such as reading, writing, thinking and talking with others about your emerging ideas (Salmona & Kaczynski, 2016); rather, they will supplement these processes. Digital tools may also help you distance (or separate) yourself from your data, helping you to appreciate what you actually see in your data rather than imposing deductive patterns in your data prematurely.

Table 2.2 lists some of the digital tools you might think about using in your research. This list is not exhaustive, just a place to start and help you on your way.

TABLE 2.2 ■ Digital Tools to Use Throughout the Process

	Digital tools
1.	Digital recordings (phone/laptop)—to capture your thoughts quickly and brain dump from time to time. Lets you "flow" without the burden of typing, spelling, punctuating etc.
2.	Online storage—It's cheap, accessible anywhere, and easy to keep running record and maintain version control.
3.	Chat logs if you interact with others over the course of a project
4.	Memos in an analogue form, electronically, or by using features of data analysis tools
5.	Microsoft To-Do (or other to-do application) in order to keep on top of your list of things to do—These lists can be shared with others in a group.
6.	PowerPoint, or other presentation application, to generate images and flow charts both for yourself and for others
7.	Mind mapping software for brainstorming and research design (refer to Section 4.A.5)
8.	Reference management tools (can be online or local). Exports can be imported in data analysis tools for literature reviews.

Take a moment to think about what digital tools you might use and remember to use them thoughtfully in your research. Consider potential ethical issues that might arise and need to be addressed in your ethics application. Also take some time to ponder your own reflexive practice in your research and how digital tools may help you in your endeavors. Remember digital tools can allow you to think more creatively about data gathering, management and analysis.

2.C.2 How Can Digital Tools Help You Move From Thinking to Writing?

Consider how you can tap into the potential of the internet to support the development of your ideas and voice with the use of blogging, wikis, and other forms of social networking to support your research. You can take this opportunity to scan for key words, concepts, viewpoints, and emerging new ideas that may help you as you develop your own thinking—that is, help you express more clearly what it is you are trying to say. Digital tools that can support the writing process within qualitative research include both individual and collaborative tools such as Google Docs, Scrivener (discussed in Section 3.B.2) and Authorea.

Most universities provide on campus and online writing center support for students. In addition, there are many open-source writing resources available for your use. This is further discussed in Section 9.B.2, *Writing a strong abstract*. A few favorite websites which are particularly helpful for qualitative writers include:

- Purdue University, Online Writing Lab (OWL): https://owl.purdue.edu/owl/purdue_owl.html
- American Psychological Association (APA): https://www.apa.org/education/grad/research
- The Writer's Handbook at the UW-Madison Writing Center: https://writing.wisc.edu/handbook/

Chapter 2 has offered ideas on how positioning yourself as a writer may assist you with starting the writing process and designing a plan of attack. This chapter has also encouraged you to give further consideration to the use of digital tools to advance your work. In the next chapter, the importance of organizing the overall direction of the writing process is considered. Strategies are offered to aid in enhancing the quality of the study and how to better communicate clearly through writing.

3 ORGANIZING YOUR WRITING

At this stage of your writing, it is likely you are recognizing the importance that the more you write the more you need to organize your work. Organization involves more than advancing drafts of writing upon which you continue to build. Organizing how you write is as important as what you write. This chapter starts with a few ideas on how to approach the task of getting organized then demonstrates building a frame for what you write by using heading styles in MS Word together with an example of free writing in Scrivener. The chapter concludes with some considerations regarding managing version control and naming conventions.

3.A PLAN TO ORGANIZE

Before you write, you need to take some time to further reflect on who you are as a writer and how you want to write. This will be different for everyone. As was mentioned in Chapter 1, some writers like to build a structure (see Section 3.B.1) and fill in this structure as they go; and some writers are more comfortable with free writing as ideas develop and start to come forward (see Section 3.B.2).

In any event, a detailed written plan is an essential element to keeping your writing on track. Wolcott (2009) emphasized the importance of having the major topics of your study identified and sequenced very early in the writing process.

> ... every author needs: a clear distinction between major points and subordinate ones and an orderly progression for presenting them. The point of this step is to develop a sequence for unfolding a story "bird by bird," not simply to get something written down. (p. 14)

These first attempts at organizing your written path need not be overly formal. Rather, approach the task of getting organized as a more open creative process of building a path to use as you navigate through the woods.

You may find diagrams and different ways of visualizing your work helpful at this point (see Chapter 4 for more on this). This early-stage plan will include identifying stepping stones where you anticipate potential murky sections. The more planning you do upfront will help in building a coherent recording of your journey.

By getting yourself organized in the early stages of the writing process you will find that you become better at taking the writing process seriously. Take some time at this point to reflect on: the intent of your writing; what your own developing style might look like; your own skills (or lack thereof); and what resources you have available. Start writing like a scholar rather than a working professional or undergrad—or worse, a cut and paste Wikipedia or ChatGPT plagiarist. You have an important task ahead as you craft your work.

Writing is a formal process which draws upon past teachings and other guidance that permeates one's thinking both as a consumer and producer of written work. For example, this time-honored reference may be drawn upon with its helpful pointers about structure and form: *The Elements of Style* (Strunk & White, 2000). Two more recent references include *On Writing Well: The Classic Guide to Writing Nonfiction* (Zinsser, 2016); and *Style: The Basics of Clarity and Grace* (Williams & Bizup, 2021). Advice, drawn from the experience of others, can be helpful by reminding you for whom you write, and how to find your own style and voice. Some valuable nuggets might include *writing by hand increases cognitive activity and makes you think; what, now what, so what; get rid of clutter; simplify, be positive, definite, concrete*; and *always read everything aloud*. In his enduring work, William Strunk Jr. (Strunk & White, 2000) emphasizes the importance of omitting needless words in writing:

> Vigorous writing is concise. A sentence should contain no unnecessary words, a paragraph no unnecessary sentences, for the same reason that a drawing should have no unnecessary lines and a machine no unnecessary parts. This requires not that the writer make all sentences short or avoid all detail and treat subjects only in outline, but that every word tell. (p. 8)

A final thought of classic wisdom to ponder is for you to *always consider yourself in your writing*. Practicing regular reflection with a lens for personal and subjective influence promotes an appropriate acknowledgement and transparency in your writing. Keep writing those memos. Most importantly, expressing your iterative writing process must include your ideas, evidence, choice of audience, and how you will deliver your work.

Now, *get going*!

There are many different ways to organize your work. You may find it helpful to develop a rough draft of a table of contents now with the understanding that it will be under continual revision OR you may enjoy free writing sections as you go and capturing fresh ideas as they occur. There is no right or wrong way to do this—find what works for you. This next section (3.B) first provides detailed steps using MS Word to build a table of contents which is easily updated as you write, and second, a way to free write your ideas using Scrivener.

3.B BUILDING A ROAD MAP: STRUCTURING YOUR THINKING

Maximizing impact is fundamental to the value of your work. A critical consideration is that the outcome of your work will be evaluated by others in regard to impact. As you begin to write, come up with a working definition of what impact means to you and decide on key criteria for evaluation. Then ask yourself—How will your writing achieve this and, how will you structure your writing so that it can effectively deliver your message and connect to your audience?

3.B.1 Creating a Frame for Your Work

As you are organizing your writing, you may find it helpful to create a table of contents as a structure, or frame, for your developing work. Having these boundaries early on may help you to stay focused, although remember this structure will change as your work develops. You can then fill in this structure one section at a time as you find inspiration to do so. Following are some ideas on how to approach this process and dealing with some hurdles you might encounter along the way. Digital tools that you can use to help you create the actual written framework for your research are ubiquitous. For the purposes of this discussion, MS Word 2019 is used to take you through the process and help frame the discussion around headings and why they matter.

There are many features you can use in MS Word (and other such software) to help you structure your writing. MS Word contains many predefined styles, used for any repetitive feature in your document, which can be applied to certain characters or paragraphs. You can use styles for headings in your documents, setting a particular style a top-level heading (**Heading 1**) and a different style for subsequent sub-headings e.g., (*Heading 2, Heading 3* and so on). Here heading styles are chosen based on for their importance, or hierarchy, in the document. You can also use styles for other repetitive headings or titles such as for example, (Insert Figure ** here) can be set as a style in a document that you can then use every time you need that particular text. Note: styles can contain definitions for a wide range of format commands such as line height, tabs, fonts, paragraph spacing, or indentation. You can find styles in the Home tab, and can use them as provided, or alter them to suit your customized work.

Once you have your style, you will find that headings are a great way to begin writing. You can use headings and their different heading levels to create a document framework from your literature map (this is demonstrated in an example at the end of this section). Applying this organizational strategy allows you to create and see the structure of your document using the Navigation pane in the View tab. This allows you to hyperlink and drop ideas into your document, and it allows you to be more efficient as you work to standardize your formatting. For additional pointers on how to apply headings in your document search online for MS Word heading styles.

Headings help your reader navigate your writing, and using heading styles in MS Word means you can build a table of contents, reorganize your document, and reformat its design without having to go through and change everything manually. To create a heading in MS Word,

1. Select the text you want to use as a heading
2. On the Home tab, move the pointer to the Styles gallery and select the heading level you want to use
3. Styles control font size, color, and spacing

You may find it helpful to build your document framework first using heading levels, however you might prefer to write first and then use styles later to format your work. There is no right way to do this; just find what works for you.

Headings are also very important when making your work accessible to others. Headings matter and can really help those with disabilities trying to access your work. Screen reader users will be able to hear which blocks of text are under which headings, and what level each heading occupies in reference to the document hierarchy; and screen reader users will also be able to skim the page by moving from heading to heading.

In summary, headings matter.

1. Headings allow your readers to navigate your work more easily.
2. Heading styles save time because you can apply consistent formatting through your work.

3. You can change the formatting of all your headings at any given level at one time.

4. You can insert an automatic table of contents easily, including page numbers, based on your headings.

5. In the outline view, you can rearrange your document by dragging headings.

6. The Navigation pane allows you to move to any part of the document by clicking its heading (live link) on the list to navigate your document. You can also search within your document and reorganize your document from the navigation pane.

The title of your work is intended to grab the attention of the reader; and your opening first sentence will continue to hold this attention. In this same way, headings and subheadings help the reader scan the pages to see if anything else captures attention. These signposts help retain your readers' engagement, improve the structure and organization of your document, and strengthens the overall readability of your work.

Any discussion about headings must include consideration about the developing hierarchy in your document framework. Headings can have many levels: section heading (Heading 1), subsection heading (Heading 2), and so on. Not only do headings matter, but where you put your headings in the hierarchy also matters. A readers must be able to skim the headings and see your story arc. Subheadings tell part of the story of the parent heading, and play a role in capturing and holding the reader's attention as they scan your document. Scanning from one subheading to the next helps guide the reader down the page. As you develop your heading hierarchy, you are actually developing how your story will be told.

> Helpful subheadings need to be Relevant, Useful, Succinct, Specific, and Unique. They summarize your work by breaking it into readable sections, so there must always be a natural flow from one subheading to the next.

When you use heading styles in your document, you can also use the automatic table of contents (ToC) feature. This allows you and your reader to scan your document structure quickly and easily, and to update it with one click when you make changes.

To update your ToC in MS Word with correct page numbers and any heading text changes:

- Right click on the ToC.
- Select *Update Field* and the following pop-up will appear:

> **Update Table of Contents**
>
> Select one of the following options:
> - ● Update page numbers only
> - ○ Update entire table
>
> Cancel | **OK**

- The first option updates page numbers
- The second option updates page numbers and headings

A digital ToC is an amazing tool for facilitating the thinking to writing process. It is a dynamic and transparent map allowing to see your developing process and thinking. Building your arguments around the use of headings (and notes to self in these headings) allow you to glance at how the flow of your thinking is making smooth transitions into written form. It can also show you how the structure of your developing argument and story arc is shaping up. This iterative perspective shift from the detailed writing to the overall structure of the presentation is a valuable exercise. Is the emerging framework what you intended? Will the internal format and words you use resonate with your target audience? Further, the ToC is dynamic and thus, when you wish to review or revise certain sections of your work, it allows you to navigate to those specific locations in the document instantly. Finally, documenting the evolution of your ToC via a series of periodic snapshots can illustrate your developing thinking into a storyboard. You can then review and narrow your final arguments and clarify how you will frame them in your finished work.

This section now finishes with an example showing a document framework being developed. Using the literature review map, following as Figure 3.1 (also presented later as Figure 4.4 when discussing mapping ideas), the table of contents in Figure 3.2 is created using headings and subheadings taken from this map. See Chapter 4 for a detailed discussion about mapping ideas and visualizing your thinking.

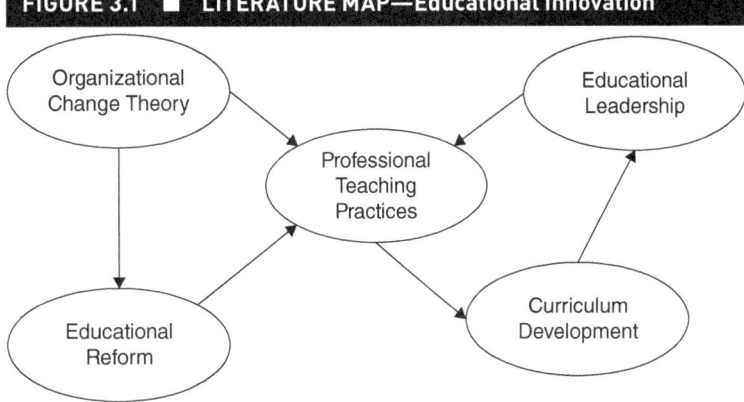

FIGURE 3.1 ■ LITERATURE MAP—Educational Innovation

FIGURE 3.2 ■ Example Table of Contents

2.0 LITERATURE REVIEW (Heading 1)

2.1 Organizational change theory (Heading 2)
    2.1.1 Oragnziational culture (Heading 3)
    2.1.2 Forces for change

2.2 Educational reform
    2.2.1 Teaching pedagogies
    2.2.2 Classroom management
    2.2.3 Student retention

2.3 Professional teaching practices

2.4 Curriculum development

2.5 Educational leadership

3.0 METHODOLOGY

The map gives five headings that can be used for a literature review section—remembering that it is most helpful to have these headings appear in the document in an order that will help to tell the story. The literature review elements shown in Figure 3.2 are Organizational Change Theory, Educational Reform, Professional Teaching Practices, Curriculum Development, and Educational Leadership. Figure 3.2 shows what an extract of your developing table of contents might look like.

Having discussed how to build a framework for your study using headings as a structure as the first step to defining your study, consider how to use free writing to capture your ideas as a different first step. Remember these organizational tools are ideas and examples; take away from these tools what works for you—start with a heading structure; start with free writing or a blend of these two different approaches OR find another way. Find something that works for you to get you started and keep you going with you writing.

3.B.2 Free Writing to Capture Ideas

Wolcott (2009) recommends that a helpful strategy for anyone whose style is evolving is simply "to let the words flow: make no corrections, check no spelling or references, don't even reread when you are on a roll" (p. 22). If the ideas in Section 3.B.1, using a more structured approach to writing, don't work for you, try free writing as an alternative.

For the purposes of this discussion, Scrivener (n.d.) is used as an example of a digital tool that can help you with organizing, editing, and planning your writing, and setting goals tracking your progress. This tool is used as an app that you download to your device. It can be used both offline and online and will save locally to your computer and to the cloud.

Scrivener is a writing aid that can help you get going by giving you some strategies for overcoming any fear you may have of the blank page. It does not do the writing for you; rather, it helps you by allowing you to arrange and organize your free-floating ideas. Creating unstructured drafts can help you develop material you can use to keep going with your writing and start creating your work on that blank page. You can compose your text in any order, break up your sections in any way that works for you. In whatever format ideas come to you, you can write about them as they emerge and develop. If you don't know where it fits into your story yet, it doesn't matter; write about your idea, as a short text or long text, and then find its place in your work later as your story develops.

Scrivener can work both as an alternative to Microsoft Word or in combination with Word. Using this tool helps writers to embrace their creative process by including features such as the following:

- a corkboard outlining tool (see Figure 3.3)
- virtual index cards

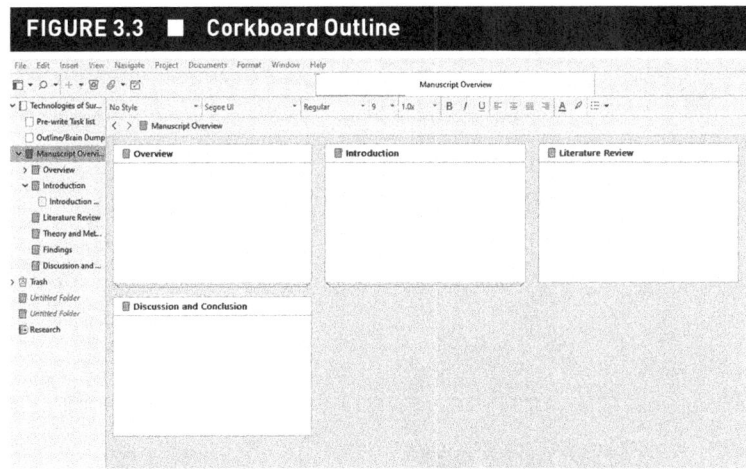

FIGURE 3.3 ■ Corkboard Outline

- dedicated folders for various subsections of a document or research notes
- a composition mode that frees your screen from distractions

Writers can also turn toward Scrivener for writing accountability, which can be very helpful for new writers. It is very important as you are developing good writing habits that you find different ways to hold yourself accountable toward achieving your goals. Make sure that you are setting yourself achievable goals and thus promoting your objective of successful writing. Scrivener allows you to

- set daily and project-based writing goals (see Figure 3.4)
- track progress, and
- see your writing history

Scrivener will help you organize your notes, ideas, and research and allow you to integrate them in different ways. For example, you may have the outline of a section available, as a guide to keep your writing on track or topic. In this example, there is also a notes view that allows you to make annotations or take notes to self. You may also include long-form information to reference as you write.

Both Microsoft Word and Scrivener are technological tools which you can use to enhance your writing skills. As you decide how far you want to integrate these tools into your own writing, you may find it helpful to

32 Qualitative Research Writing

FIGURE 3.4 ■ Project Writing Targets

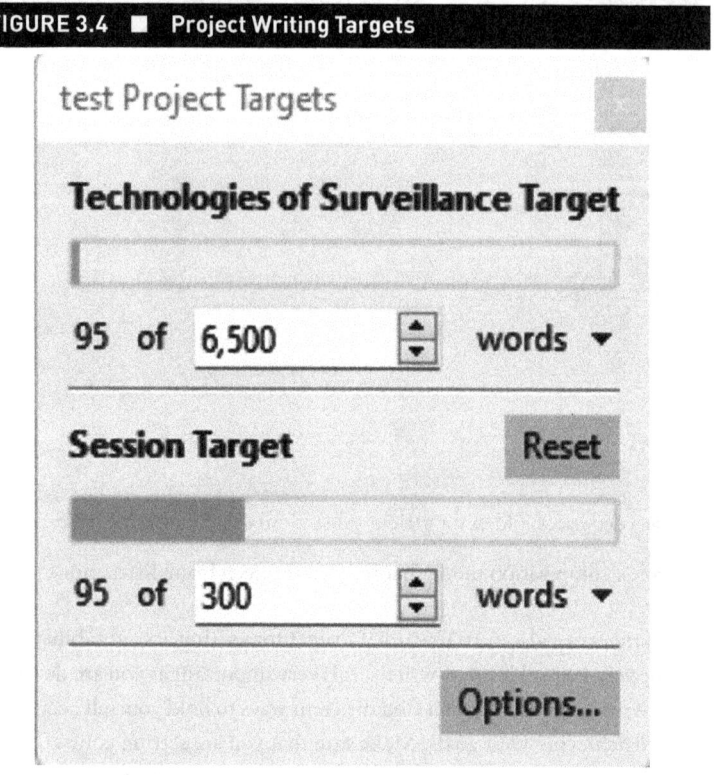

consider the barriers of ease of use and usefulness. If you don't perceive a technological tool as easy to use and useful, you are less likely to be successful in adopting the tool (Salmona & Kaczynski, 2016). A central tenant when considering adoption of any technology is to always consider that these are only tools. You are the craftsperson, how you employ such tools and control their use is entirely up to you. Now, it is time to think about version control and saving all versions of your work.

3.C SAVING EVERYTHING

Saving everything as you go and managing version control of your documents matters. Here are some tips about how to keep track of your work.

3.C.1 Version Control and Saving Everything

As you write you will continually develop your thinking. Instead of changing one document all the time, create a new version of the document each time you improve your work. Keep everything safely stored as you never know when you will want to go back to an earlier version. When you realize that you are going off track or you are developing an idea that is not working out, you can go back to a prior version and start a new path, or perhaps as your thinking is developing you may realize that some of your earlier discarded work is now relevant and needs to be included. Also, there may come a time when you, or someone else, actually deletes something which you can luckily recover from an earlier version.

Create your own version control system for managing your writing. Typically, version control is used in teams for tracking individual changes made by each team member and helping to prevent conflicts in concurrent work. This is particularly important as changes made in one part of the document might clash with those made by another team member at the same time. Version control in a document helps you to make sure that you are working in the current iteration of the master document.

As you make changes in your writing, you can save new versions of the document and keep the old ones.

Another strategy would be for you to save a document every time by giving it a new name so that you can always go back and see what change you have made in the past. Manual document control can be done with a naming convention or by adding a table at the beginning of the document that says the version, the author and a brief summary of the changes in that version and the date the changes were made.

> NOTE: If you are using Google Drive, this strategy of saving successive written versions won't work as Google Drive does not allow you to save previous versions of documents. All amendments are saved in the document on Google Drive as you work. If you wanted to save your prior work, you would have to save any changes or new writing as a new document.

3.C.2 Naming Convention

Come up with a document naming convention that allows you to find particular work when you need to. There are many ways to do this, so develop something that makes sense, and will work, for you. Make sure that any document naming convention you use is easy to follow and, therefore, useful. Avoid anything obscure or cryptic and keep it practical, for example, all draft documents might end with a *D*.

> A simple convention you might use could be
> DATE_PROJECT NAME_ABBREVIATED TITLE_VERSION NUMBER
> 20210512_JA_LearningHowToWrite_V1.5
> This document name would describe a journal article you are writing called "Learning How to Write" and that this particular version is Version 1.5 created on May 12, 2021. In this case, by putting Year, then Month, then Day, all your files will automatically sort in date order.

It is also a great idea to put this File Name in the header or footer of every page and on the cover sheet, so that you are able to see instantly which document you are looking at.

When you are creating a naming convention brevity is important. Keep the file name as short as possible, use plain English to describe the content in the file name and make sure to avoid names such as File_33. Avoid using blank spaces, special characters or punctuation in your file names. Think about using key words in the name as it may make the file easier to find. As your work develops, you are going to have to keep track of a lot of different versions. Try everything you can to make this as easy as possible.

> Go to Stanford Libraries at https://www.library.stanford.edu and search for "best practices file naming" to find out what works for you. There you will find their guides including: *Data Best Practices and Case Studies*. You will find some great resources about how to name files (manage your research data), along with case studies and examples.

Something else you can do is to create a table at the beginning of the document to capture all the changes in a particular document as they are made. The table will grow with each document as changes are made and recorded. An example of a table documenting changes is shown in Table 3.1. Here initial drafts are numbered 0.1, 0.2, 0.3, and so on. Once the first document draft has been

TABLE 3.1 ■ Version Control Table

Version	Date	Changes Made
0.1	1 May 2023	First draft of outline
0.2	9 May 2023	First review with feedback from colleague
0.3	15 May 2023	Incorporated feedback from colleague and further developed analysis section

completed, you might change the document numbering to 1.0, 1.1, or 1.2, with any major update after that labelled as 2.0. Using this process, you have numbers and dates to refer to find earlier work. Remember to keep all drafts and versions of your work as separate documents, safely stored for any future review.

3.C.3 Keeping Track of References

One of your most laborious and tricky tasks is to keep track of all your references. If you ask 10 different people how best to do this, you will probably receive 10 different answers. Again, find the way that works best for you.

Managing, organizing and citing references can sometimes be really challenging, particularly if you haven't kept good records tracking what sources you are citing. It is absolutely soul destroying to come to the end of your write-up and have a messy list of references with missing references, page numbers, publication dates. Even worse is having to find the actual source for a quotation included in your work.

You can go "old-school" and create index cards for all the work you want to cite. Another simple method is to email yourself links of online articles, websites, and online databases that you are thinking of using in your research work. References can be handled manually, but using a reference management tool will give you greater flexibility and productivity.

Software programs and online application tools can help you keep track of your literature and provide efficient workflow management of your references. These digital tools will help you stay focused on your research write-up. It is easy to find a wide range of these reference management tools which can be used for organizing, managing, and creating references and citations. Some of these tools are available to the user free, and others require an upfront payment. Remember to check your university library to see what they have available free to students and academics. Examples include, in no particular order RefWorks, Mendeley, Zotero, Endnote, and EasyBib.

Having spent time thinking about your research, now it is time to consider effective ways to present your writing. Chapter 4 introduces strategies on the application of visuals in the writing process.

4 VISUALIZING YOUR WRITING

Now that you are underway with your thinking and writing, it is time to start visualizing how and what this thinking represents. Visualizing your thinking can help you to see things in a different way, which can give you valuable insight into how your thinking is developing as you refine each new writing draft version.

An example of visualizing is the use of a concept map to establish parameters around the scope of a study and building connections between the key elements. Visualizing may also involve drawing a graphical literature map of key search terms used during the literature review process. In both of these examples, mapping provides a valuable strategy to aid the researcher in staying on track and avoid getting lost in the many potentially distracting paths emerging during the writing process.

This chapter discusses the benefits of finding ways to visualize the connections in your work:

1. Keeping a visual diary or map of the main concepts framing your research

2. How you may further refine these concepts as you progress through the study

3. Using figures to strengthen your message

It also suggests the following:

1. Drawing key terms and concepts on a whiteboard with directional symbols to aid in building a starting map

2. Using this visual to guide your writing and strengthen key components that frame your research

4.A COMMUNICATING RESEARCH THINKING THROUGH MAPS

Consider how the many paths in your research story fit together. Visualizing the thinking behind your writing can help you do this. You do not have to be artistic to be successful here. Diagrams, figures, and flowcharts are visual examples of research maps which can be created in many different ways. Just think of visualizing as communicating with symbols rather than words.

4.A.1 What Are Research Maps?

Sharing your paths of inquiry through visuals can be very helpful to both you and your intended reading audience. The process of building visuals can help you identify broken links in your thinking and also expose overlooked paths of inquiry not taken. There are many types of visualizing approaches recognized in social science research. In this chapter, the following five types of visualizations are discussed:

1. Concept maps
2. Literature maps
3. Mind maps
4. Argument maps
5. Logic models

After this discussion, Section 4.C presents an example using maps. The research paper is offered as an illustration to demonstrate the blending of three visualization approaches which are discussed in this Section 4.A: beginning with a mind map, then moving forward with a concept map, and concluding with a working draft of a literature map.

These types of visualizations represent a few of the more popular variations of graphics to help you organize, structure, and succinctly display important aspects of a research study. Note that these variations in visualization share both similarities and distinct differences. Each of the five examples serve unique roles in a research study. Although each example is unique, maps generally use positioning and size of components, types of connections and key terms to indicate importance and closeness of association (Stake, 2010, p. 107). Your choice of which type of map to use in a particular section of your writing will therefore be determined based upon appropriate alignment with the overall intended use in your research study.

4.A.2 How to Start Making a Map

Capturing your thinking using visuals may feel very overwhelming. Remember, you do not have to be artistic to be successful visualizing your research writing. Start by capturing your thoughts in any form that feels comfortable for you: doodle on a napkin, use a whiteboard to rough sketch a storyboard, or write on the back of an envelope. It doesn't matter—just capture what you are thinking in a drawing, or doodle, and give consideration to how you can visualize it.

Making maps relies on your identification and linking of key words. As an activity try brainstorming some of the key words you use to describe important aspects of your study and for online searches of literature. The following resources are two helpful tools to identify and refine key words:

1. Princeton University offers WordNet Search, an online lexical database tool which you can use for ideas as you explore linkages and relationships (WordNet, 2010).

2. A helpful site for brainstorming word clouds is available through MonkeyLearn, (n.d.) an online tool that uses text analysis models to automatically tag your text. Tagging can help you visualize the connections in, and develop insights about, your key words.

Brainstorming key concepts can also be facilitated using online images. A technique which you may find helpful is to use an online image search engine. There are several image search engines available online. When using one of these resources you will need to begin your image search with variations of the key words from your study. A popular image browser is Google Images (n.d.). The Advanced Image Search option offers even more detailed commands to further refine and customize your search. This option is accessible in the settings function once you begin your image search. As you browse the search results, draw upon various images for creative ideas on how to visualize what you are attempting to capture and share with your reader.

4.A.3 Concept Maps

Making a concept map involves identifying key words and terms which frame your investigation into the issues around the social problem which your study explores. These terms represent key concepts and central ideas which share common meanings relevant to your writing. This in turn helps you frame your thinking and clarify what is central to your research. You may find it helpful to write each key term on a Post-it Note then move the terms around while you consider

TABLE 4.1 ■ Making a Concept Map

	Making a Concept Map
1.	Brainstorm a key word for each main concept of your study
2.	Verify the concept list includes the main topic, social problem, and all key issues
3.	Mix and move the key words around as you consider different relationships
4.	Determine levels of importance and proximity among key words
5.	Extend each main concept with lines to related concepts; this promotes lateral thinking
6.	Make connections or graphically associate all key words
7.	Save the map as a draft version, subject to refinements as you move forward with writing

relevant connections between each note. Once you have these key terms organized, try different connections with the concepts and central ideas as a strategy to expand your options and to explore alternative pathways of inquiry (Table 4.1).

A more thorough discussion on concept maps may be reviewed in the following:

Martelo, M. L. (2011). Use of bibliographic systems and concept maps: Innovative tools to complete a literature review. *Research in the Schools, 18*(1), 62–70.

Novak, J. D. & Canas, A. J. (2008). *The theory underlying concept maps and how to construct and use them* (Technical Report IHMC Cmap Tools 2006-01 Rev 01-2008). Florida Institute for Human and Machine Cognition.

Stake, R. E. (2010). *Qualitative research: Studying how things work.*: Guilford Press. **[Concept Mapping, pp. 106–109]**

Wilson, J., Mandich, A., & Magalhães, L. (2016). Concept mapping: A dynamic, individualized and qualitative method for eliciting meaning. *Qualitative Health Research, 26*(8), 1151–1161.

4.A.4 Literature Maps

Reporting on your review of literature is an essential part of the academic writing process. Your selections of scholarly books and peer-reviewed journal articles represent the construction of an intentional path of inquiry which you are developing. A review of literature offers informed insights beyond your current understandings, and hopefully encourages you to consider suggestions by other authors to build upon and extend their research (Machi & McEvoy, 2016; Piantanida & Garman, 2012).

As you dig into the literature you are shaping your own path of inquiry which is clarified and framed through a process which is unique for every study. These choices form a foundation for the thinking behind your research design and the supporting argument to the message which you intend to convey through your study. The construction of a literature map can help you be clear when sharing this foundational thinking with your audience (Table 4.2).

Before building a literature map, review and organize your selected literature into digital folders which are labeled by key terms. Begin this step by establishing a consistent naming convention for each PDF research article. Place articles which share a common concept into appropriate folders. Maintain an updated reference listing of all article citations. Maintaining a master documents folder on your computer is common practice, however, as your review of literature expands this approach can be overly labor intensive. There are a wide range of digital tools which can be used to aid in organizing and storing your literature review citations and annotated bibliographies. Some of these applications include Endnote, Mendeley, RefWorks, Zotero, Papers, Bookends, and CMS which functions as a virtual filing cabinet (Fink, 2019, p. 34). Another option to manage your literature review documents is the use of a qualitative data analysis software program (QDAS). Many of these qualitative research software programs and applications provide data management features which support literature review management. A few examples include Dedoose, NVivo, ATLAS.ti, and MAXQDA. Regardless of the digital tool resources you use to organize your literature, having ready access to your personal library of literature will benefit the quality and efficiency of your writing. This initial step of organizing your literature into folders of common concepts also benefits your writing by allowing you to use folder labels to help build a literature map.

TABLE 4.2 ■ Making a Literature Map

Making a Literature Map	
1.	Review the main themes raised from the literature review
2.	Identify where different authors share agreement on important concepts related to your study
3.	Identify where the different authors disagree on important concepts
4.	Examine where important concepts share common relationships
5.	Classify and group the main themes
6.	Align the main themes and address gaps and disagreements
7.	Expand and link the main themes into a network of connections forming a map

A more thorough discussion on literature maps may be reviewed in the following:

Desai, V., Potter, R. B., & Potter, R. (2006). *Doing development research.* SAGE.
   [Literature Reviews and Bibliographic Searches, pp. 210–220]
Machi, L. A. & McEvoy, B. T. (2016). *The literature review: Six steps to success* (3rd ed.). SAGE.

4.A.5 Mind Maps

Imagine mind mapping as watching a box of ping pong balls thrown into a room and bouncing all around. Just to make this more challenging, the ping pong balls are different colors and sizes. Now consider that the room is your mind, and the box of bouncing ping pong balls are the ideas you have about the research topic you are writing about. Mind mapping captures these bouncing ideas into some visual order (Table 4.3). The process involves building visual, nonlinear representations of ideas and their relationships to create a flowing association of ideas. This process is intended to promote free-form spontaneous thinking to stimulate creativity (Biktimirov & Nilson, 2006; Davies, 2011). A limitation of such an open flowing interaction of ideas is the challenge of imposing order and structure to shifting complex thoughts and their web of relationships among numerous key concepts. Used in concert with concept maps, however, the less precise and open mind mapping strategy may stimulate unique paths of inquiry which can then be more carefully examined using a more formal concept map.

TABLE 4.3 ■ Making a Mind Map	
Making a Mind Map	
1.	Start with a box of ping pong balls—oops, bad idea.
2.	Play a game of ping pong and brainstorm. Any game will work; the point is to have some fun. Throw a Frisbee or toss balls of paper into a wastebasket. Try playing with your less dominant hand to make sure you are having fun and not being too competitive.
3.	Open your thinking and strive to be inductive while pondering the social problem which your writing is addressing. Make notes as you go and consider what if.
4.	Map your notes and their relationships to create a flowing association of ideas.

A more thorough discussion on mind maps may be reviewed in the following:

Davies, M. (2011). Concept mapping, mind mapping and argument mapping: what are the differences and do they matter? *Higher Education 62*(3), 279–301.

4.A.6 Argument Maps

"Argument mapping allows students to display inferential connections between propositions and contentions, and to evaluate them in terms of validity of argument structure and the soundness of argument premises" (Davies, p. 280, 2011). A logical argument involves the presentation of statements or premises and claims or conclusions which are used to form a line of reasoning which you lay out in your writing (Table 4.4). Your intended audience must be able to follow this line to a reasoned conclusion which is accepted as credible and trustworthy. Your argument map can be used to visually lay out this path of reasoning.

In qualitative research the intent is not to present if then causal inferences. Rather, a qualitative study is designed to provide a path to deeper insights which illuminate and explore nuanced multiple meanings. A modified form of an argument map can be adopted in qualitative writing by avoiding the application of causal inferences and emphasizing the visual inductive complexity of shared relationships.

A more thorough discussion on argument maps may be reviewed in the following:

TABLE 4.4 ■ Making an Argument Map

Making an Argument Map

1.	Review the focus statement or central question of the study
2.	Select key words that frame the focus statement
3.	Review each research question of the study and select representative key words
4.	Refer to study key findings and select representative key words
5.	Form key words into a line of reasoning map (multiple meanings may show divergent paths)

Hirschheim R., Murungi, D. M., & Pena, S. (2012). Witty invention or dubious fad? Using argument mapping to examine the contours of management fashion. *Information and Organization, 22*(1), 60–84.

4.A.7 Logic Models

A logic model is commonly used to visualize connections between a social problem and how processes are employed by a program to improve performance and solve the problem. In a related sense, a logic model is a visual method of presenting a key idea and exploring the elements surrounding this idea (Table 4.5). These elements are generally grouped into four processes; input, activities, output, and outcome (Fitzpatrick et al., 2011; Knowlton & Phillips, 2013). Building a visual logic model involves the identification of activities in each of the four processes. This approach offers several benefits such as helping fill in what is occurring around a social problem and that which is missing or not being addressed. By building a visual thread of evidence-based logic the model can aid in untangling and clarifying complex relationships. In a visual format this information can stimulate careful consideration of the relationship between activities and outcomes. In qualitative writing, such a model could be employed to draw graphical attention to important elements which are highlighted in the text.

A more thorough discussion on logic models may be reviewed in the following:

Kalu, M., & Norman, K. (2018). Step by step process from logic model to case study method as an approach to educational programme evaluation. *Global Journal of Educational Research, 17*(1), 73–85.

Knowlton, L. W. & Phillips, C. C. (2013). *The logic model guidebook: Better strategies for great results* (2nd ed.). SAGE.

TABLE 4.5 ■ Making a Logic Model	
Making a Logic Model	
1.	Identify the social forces which **input** or define the issue or problem you are exploring
2.	Identify what **activities** define the focus and research questions of your study
3.	Identify **outputs** (who is doing what, etc.) which result from these activities
4.	Determine the immediate and long-term **outcomes** or changes which are anticipated
5.	Build a linear map with connections to each of these four processes

4.B USING MAPS TO VISUALIZE YOUR WRITING

Developing connections and showing diagrammatic relationships between ideas is a formative process intended to promote ongoing refinement throughout your writing. Each version of a visual map builds upon and refines this thinking into a unique trail upon which you can expand to strengthen your study. A strong trail allows you to review the paths you took to reach where you are now; it helps you remember how you got here. Knowing this will help you build stronger arguments; and having a more cohesive story line will help your audience follow you on your journey. Keep each version of these evolving maps as an audit trail as you further develop your thinking. That way you can always go back and review how you advanced your research thinking (remember what we covered in Chapter 3.C.1 about version control as you develop your work). You may find it helpful to post a paper copy of your visual drafts on the wall near your writing work area as a reminder of the path you are building through your writing.

> These evolving maps also promote ongoing visual brainstorming to further extend insights.

A strategy which you may find helpful when exploring relationships among key concepts and key terms is to try different types of lines used in forming connections (refer to Figure 4.1). A straight solid line is commonly used when first making a connection. Consider how the visual meaning of this connection changes when a different type of line is made. Curved lines and circles have different connotations from a straight line. By substituting a dashed line for a solid line, the visual meaning is further altered. A thicker line implies greater significance than a thin line. Applying directional arrows to connections and bi-directional arrows also refines the intended visual message. The important point in this discussion about using lines to build relationships and connections is for you to explore and experiment with new connections as you advance your writing.

Another strategy to promote visual brainstorming is to experiment with different templates for your key terms. Consider adopting templates from diverse disciplines including education, health sciences, software design, project management, business data flow models, or an organizational chart. A quick starting source for sample templates can be found by searching Google Images (n.d.). Templates offer a different way to visually shape and define how you build connections in your study. More complex and

46 Qualitative Research Writing

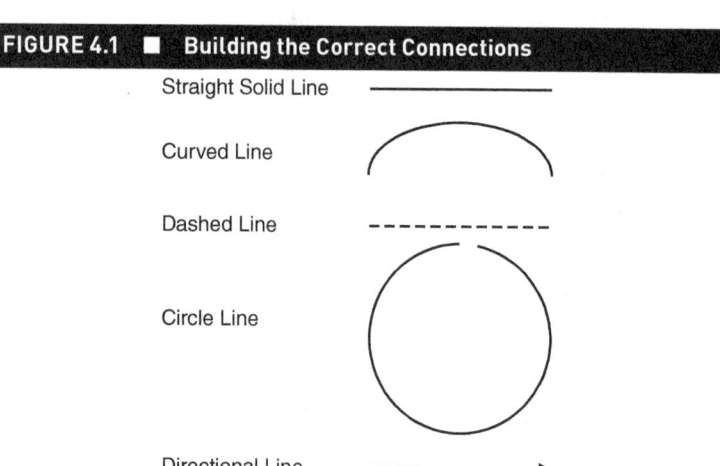

FIGURE 4.1 ■ Building the Correct Connections

advanced templates are available in a wide range of software programs and digital applications. Microsoft Word supports inserting pictures, shapes, and charts into a document. Microsoft Power Point provides compatible features which can be used to build and refine figures and diagrams. In addition to Microsoft Word, Microsoft Power Point, and Google Images (n.d.), there are a wide range of dedicated programs and applications available to support digital building. A few popular examples include Microsoft Vizio, Lucidchart, SmartDraw, ConceptDraw Diagram, Gliffy, Edraw Max, VisualParadigm Online, and open source IHMC CmapTools. This brief listing of software programs and digital applications is not intended to be comprehensive, rather to inform you that there are many available resources ranging from simple to complex which you can use in building and displaying visual research maps to enhance your writing.

Visualizing through graphic image building can also be used to overcome possible inertia in your writing. Overcoming initial uncertainty with visualizations is much like trying to figure out what the first sentence is for your writing. Consider how you might begin writing about your research. Where do you begin? The skills needed in overcoming the challenges of building this first visualization is much the same. Your goal here is to connect relevant content by effectively communicating relevant connections visually.

> Both visualizing and writing begin much the same—have a clear understanding of the key concept which frames your research inquiry.

Identification of the keywords is a helpful first step to structure and guide an inquiry such as yours. Refer to Table 4.6 for suggestions on how to select the most appropriate keywords.

Once major key words are identified, the writer composes or refines the purpose summary and a succinct focus statement. Refer to Chapter 1, Section 1.B.1, for a discussion on writing up the study focus and purpose statements; also see Section 4.C for an example using a focus statement as a starting point for developing a study design.

Accurately expressing your study intentions requires time as the narrative is fine tuned to best express the writers aim. It is normal to compose and refine several drafts at this stage. Strive to express the key idea of your study, and experiment by mixing and matching terms to see what fits best to describe the central idea of the study. Who, what, when, where, or how opens different doors into the inquiry. Which door gets you closer to what you seek? Trying out different action verbs also helps to open up diverse paths and determine what works best. Does your study explore, investigate, discover, tell the story of, or seek to better understand? You may be surprised to find that by trying a different term you become better at expressing what it is your study is about.

As well as maps, you may find that diagrams, charts, and tables are also effective at conveying your message succinctly. A wide range of figures are available, each offering a unique way of expressing a particular point you wish to emphasize. Descriptions of data such as the demographics of your research setting can be

TABLE 4.6 ■ Identifying and Exploring Keywords

Identifying and Exploring Keywords	
1.	Identify the key concept of your research
2.	Write this key concept on a whiteboard and circle it
3.	Next write down the social forces affecting this key concept
4.	Is there an order to these social forces or are some of these elements encompassing?
5.	Erase and rework the social forces to better express your intended research purpose
6.	Finally, add connections and directional symbols to aid in clarifying key connections
7.	Identify any important social forces which do not fit or have been excluded
8.	Make sure you take a picture of your whiteboard when you finish

succinctly shown numerically using a chart. Occurrences of overlapping events could be visualized using a code co-occurrence table. Regardless of the type of figure used, note that highlighting important insights can enhance your writing. Using a visual interpretation must be accompanied with written interpretation so that your condensed visual message is fully understood. The following resources provide ideas on how to use figures and tables to present complicated information in a way that is accessible and understandable to your reader:

- Using visuals to support your writing process, Methodspace post (Hooper, n.d.)
- Figures and charts handout (Writing Center, University of North Carolina at Chapel Hill, n.d.)
- Using graphic organizers for writing essays, summaries and research blog (Nishadha, 2021)
- Analysis charts, tables, and plots in the Dedoose User Guide (Dedoose Support Team, 2021)

4.C AN EXAMPLE USING MAPS

The following research paper is provided as an example to demonstrate the blending of three visualization approaches featured earlier in this chapter. In this example, the researchers began by building a mind map then moved forward with a concept map and concluded with a working draft of a literature map. Also notice how a focus statement and a purpose statement were used to introduce the writers thinking behind the story arc.

EDUCATIONAL LEADERSHIP AND THE FORCES OF CHANGE: A FRAMEWORK FOR PROMOTING COMMUNITY ENGAGEMENT (KACZYNSKI & SALMONA, 2023)

Introduction

The focus of this study explores a better understanding of successful educational leadership when addressing organizational change by engaging with change at the community level. The purpose of the study recognizes that the process of change is seen here as ongoing shifts between decline and advancement of organizational practices. Remember the phrase, "Don't change it if it isn't broken." Another example from pop culture may also apply, when the head of Harry Potter's school says, "Progress for the sake of progress must be discouraged" (Rowling, 2003); troubling times lay ahead. As an educational leader, resisting the forces of change, at the very least, promotes organizational stagnation. When an organization remains stagnant and frozen, regrettably those who seek innovation often become disillusioned, frustrated, and ultimately disconnected. A theoretical framework to explore the forces driving change is used in this study to recognize and respond to power networks of relationships which are constantly in tension (Foucault, 1977, p. 26). Deeper insights can be gained by investigating these power networks at play in the education organization and community which are recognized to promote or hinder change. Thus, by deconstructing forces of change within the educational organization the indicators of fixed or frozen tension can be unpacked and constructively reformed.

In an effort to move out of a frozen state and promote growth, a three-step action process of advancing organizational development through change management may be adopted. This process entails unfreezing, implanting a change then refreezing practices (Cummings et al., 2016; Lewin, 1947). Planning and implementing an organizational change process offers a constructive alternative to flowing with frozen social power networks. In essence, the purpose of the study acknowledges that change happens, like it or not. The following three questions are used to further explore this dynamic:
- How do educational leaders do their best to unfreeze a social power network (Foucault, 1977)?
- How can resistance to change be unpacked at the organizational and community level?
- What is needed to build a framework to successfully pursue organizational transformation?

Theoretical Framework

Sociologists define social change as shifts in human interactions and relationships that transform cultural and social institutions. Major social shifts, driven by change, occur over time and often have profound and long-term consequences for society (Knight & Sened, 2001). More incremental change occurs at the organizational level. Organizations generally change to provide value to a new set of rules providing directions on how to govern society (Coccia, 2018).

Five commonly recognized social institutions which are encountered at the community level are the family, the state or government, business, education, and religion (see Figure 4.2). Additional social institutions may include law, health care, mass media, technology, and the military.

As educational leaders participate in organizational change practices, they increasingly are drawn into community engagement involving these

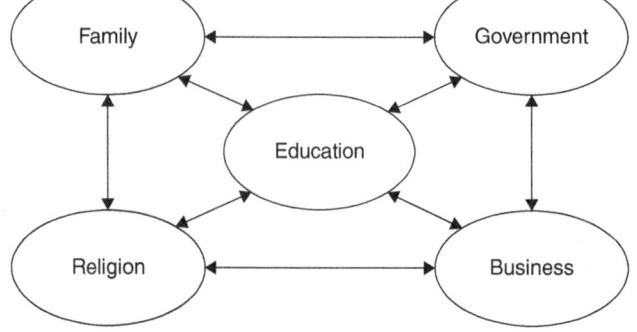

various social institutions. Influencing the change process, and strategic planning, are instrumental steps for successful education leaders promoting change (Farmer-Hanson et al., 2018; Fossland & Sandvoll, 2021). The strategic planning process is a deliberate approach taken to produce "fundamental decisions and action that shape and guide what an organization (or other entity) is, what it does, and why" (Bryson, 2018, p. 8). Given the constant tensions of change upon the organization, being successful requires a working approach to the change process with community social institutions. Educational leaders confronting social problems at the organizational level thus are continually challenged by community social institutions to be more transparent in demonstrating the importance of constructively engaging with the forces of change.

Engaging the community in a change process is particularly complex due to the wide range of divergent interests and aims among various social institutions. In this study, the use of two different analytic models are presented as a means to promote a mutually supportive theoretical framework for successful change. Stakeholder analysis is the first model for mapping and connecting the complexity of overlapping and competing interests. The second model is force-field analysis of the principal forces that drive change. It is interesting for educational leaders to note that these two analytic models demonstrate intersections between two different disciplines; organizational management offers a formalized approach to the study of stakeholder dynamics and organizational sociology continues to expand the use of force-field analysis. Together, these social science disciplines offer a valuable subfield perspective and provide unique insights into a mutually supportive theoretical framework with direct benefits to the discipline of educational leadership.

Conceptualizing a Framework

By advancing the theoretical framework proposed in this study, a conceptualized framework may be applied to functionally enhance best practices. The following sequential foundation is offered by the authors to demonstrate fundamental action steps educational leaders may consider when moving from theoretical to conceptual framework adoption.

1. **Change Statement**—Draft a clear and concise written statement of the change process. Provide clarity regarding what the intended goals are and the underlying drivers for change. Identify specific goals and avoid raising multiple issues. Start the process with small achievable goals from which to build success.
2. **Institutional Stakeholders**—Identify the social institutions at the local level that hold a vested stake in the change process.
3. **Institutional Capacity**—Conduct an assessment of available institutional and community resources available and relevant to driving and resisting the change process.
4. **Stakeholder Analysis**—Visually map and describe the roles of the involved stakeholders.
5. **Community Engagement**— Gather community input from stakeholders regarding their views and intentions to the change process. Promote open communication through intentional listening from all stakeholders, not just engaging with those in agreement. Facilitate a *story circle* for sharing stories on a common theme. Story threads can be woven together into shared community interests.
6. **Force-field Analysis**—Draft and map an analysis of the change process.
7. **Organizational Positioning**—Propose a recommended change for the educational institution to review for adoption.
8. **Retrench and Celebrate**—Adopt the new change in the organization and celebrate success with all stakeholders. Avoid a continuous cycle of constant change by taking a break.

This conceptual framework is offered only as a demonstration, given that each sequence will undergo considerable unique adjustments in different communities as educational leaders plan and respond to change as a dynamic and complex process. Adoption of this example of a conceptual framework should also consider that the change process will continue to evolve. As a result, the above sequence will require ongoing updates and analysis as the change statement will likely evolve over time.

Building a Framework

In this study, stakeholder analysis is broadly defined as the examination of shared interests and goals by organizations and community institutions with a vested interest or holding a stake in the outcomes of the change process. A common definition of who is a stakeholder has been contested among different disciplines. Public and nonprofit management literature has maintained a broad inclusive approach whereas business management literature has, in the past, presented a narrower and more restrictive definition (Bryson, 2004, p. 22). These distinctions, however, have increasingly evolved toward inclusivity and reflect shifting social norms promoting social justice and a greater social good (Mitchell et al., 1997). The importance of establishing a shared definition of who is a community stakeholder represents an essential first step for successfully adoption of the framework. Bryson (2004) contends that broader inclusivity promotes increased stakeholder analysis practices and organizational success with change:

> strategic management processes that employ a reasonable number of competently done stakeholder analyses are more likely to be successful – that is, meet mandates, fulfill missions and create public value – than those that do not. (p. 26)

A range of stakeholder analysis techniques may be drawn upon depending on the type of strategic change intervention being considered. A few examples include building a coalition to support innovation, monitoring and evaluating programs and services, or external funding grant development (Bryson, 2004; Bryson et al., 2011; Kellogg Foundation, 2017).

Additional steps in building an evidence-based framework include visually mapping stakeholders as interactive representatives of community social institutions. This is a useful technique for grouping shared goals and common ground. Mapping also facilitates identifying differences among community institutions regarding conflicting interests and competing outcomes (Bryson et al., 2011; Nauheimer, 1997).

In addition to stakeholder analysis, force-field analysis can be used to identify forces of tension to build a framework to unfreeze and move toward transformational educational change (Fullan, 2006; Wells, 2006). Such an intervention change process is action research driven involving direct involvement with the organization and community (Schein, 1999; Zuber-Skerritt, 2015). Force-field analysis supports refinement of the change process with expanded steps of engagement. By adopting a process which entails unfreezing, implanting a change then refreezing practices, the educational leader has the flexibility to (1) increase the drivers for change, (2) decrease the restrainers to change, and/or (3) turn a restrainer into a driver (Harvey, 1995, p. 29). Together, these steps offer the means for building an evidence-based framework for addressing organizational change by engaging with change at the community level.

Education and Community Benefits

A key benefit from this study is the promotion of transparent improvement of educational leadership practices at the community level. When educational leaders achieve a better understanding of the forces of social change, they are then better positioned to successfully promote effective multistakeholder partnerships. Through a guided constructive process of reflection, change management can be instilled among all key stakeholders for long-term success for education and the greater community.

By seeking a better understanding of the social power networks within an educational organization this theoretical discussion has shown that successful leaders must recognize these networks as an integral part of change. This is particularly relevant for educational leaders as they promote best practices in education while contending with a wide range of interrelated issues. To illustrate the complexity of these networks upon change refer to the concept map shown in Figure 4.3. As visually demonstrated, changes intended to improve student learning competencies can clearly have a ripple effect impacting other interrelated issues.

It is critically important today to constructively engage in and manage change as communities experience ongoing disrupting destructive behaviors and confront fermenting negative beliefs which now polarize many school community relationships. Finding ways to repair harms done to relationships can help position educational institutions to better meet the needs of student learners. Thus, bringing all stakeholders toward a common ground promotes positive outcomes for student learning through advances in educational practices.

Scholarly Significance

Change management is an underlying element of social science research. Research begins with a social problem. An empirical design is created and implemented to study the problem. Findings and results are drawn from the evidence. Most studies conclude with a call for future study to explore unanswered paths. Often, steps to address the problem are offered which require implementation of a change process. Regrettably, such studies fall short by offering little to achieve long-term meaningful community change.

FIGURE 4.3 ■ CONCEPT MAP—Educational Practices

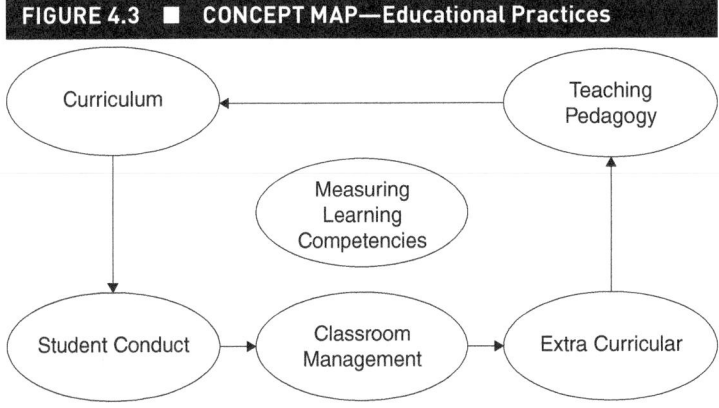

There remains an all too common gap in the research literature of current empirical practices which incorporate change management into the literature review. Change is often taken as a given and omitted and overlooked in the literature review which frames many social science studies. As visually demonstrated in Figure 4.4, organizational change theory literature provides an essential component to the literature which this study draws upon.

FIGURE 4.4 ■ LITERATURE MAP—Educational Innovation

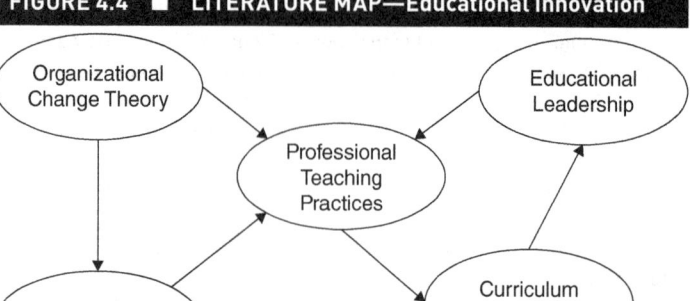

This study is offered in response to a potential fundamental weakness of current social science inquiry practices by promoting the importance of change theory. The scholarly benefits of drawing upon interdisciplinary literature on change theory has not only provided the foundation of a framework for this study but also promotes a valuable subfield perspective supporting a broader adoption of change theory into social science research.

There is an ultimate scholarly significance for promoting the application of empirical practices in change management at the organization and community level. The future advancement of society and of greater concern ". . . the future survival of the planet requires us to reimagine leadership not as the selfish pursuit of individual or group gain, but the collective commitment to building sustainable organizations and societies" (Burnes et al., 2016, p. 14). Consider the different social institutions: family, the state or government, business, education, religion, law, healthcare, mass media, technology, and the military. What is particularly significant here is that all social institutions share a common goal of strengthening communities for the future. Each in their own way are attempting to deal with the future through change management. For educational leaders, change management directly aligns with the duties of educational institutions serving the community. Consider the significance that change is fundamentally about dealing with the future. Then consider the implication that educational institutions are responsible for preparing youth for the future and in so doing shaping the future.

The above research study provides examples of using three maps to visualize changes in educational practices at the organizational level. Hopefully, the study demonstrates practical steps which benefit the overall quality of research writing. This chapter has shown how keeping a visual diary or map of the main concepts framing your research allows you to further refine key concepts and how the use of figures clarifies and strengthens your message. Chapter 5 offers some ideas about how to write about your research design.

5 WRITING ABOUT YOUR RESEARCH DESIGN

Having spent time visualizing and mapping your thinking, it is now time to write about your research design. Moving from visualizing to the formal writing process involves a transition requiring a shift in the type and style of language you are using to communicate. It is important to think about these steps as you move from the thinking and mapping stages of your work to preparing something in written form.

Writing about the connections you are building in your qualitative study design requires a clear and consistent presentation of three important elements: your theoretical approach, the study focus, and the main research questions that your study is addressing. How can researchers establish these connections in a practical way? Making connections begins with drawing upon qualitative theory in the literature to describe your own work. This is an integral part of telling your research story and allows you to then move forward with explaining the study's particular use of a qualitative theoretical framework. Theory must be woven throughout your story arc. This includes critically exploring strategies to build a convincing argument that frames and supports your use of theory as an integral part of a consistent story.

Research methods encompass all the steps you take as you go about conducting your study. Your qualitative theoretical perspective represents your methodology as you combine your theory discussions with the study research methods. Theory provides a framework for how you approach the mechanics of the inquiry. Methods are the mechanics which explain the practical steps you are taking to get the job done. In a sense, you are writing about the strategy used for your plan of attack. The study focus, central research questions, and the steps you plan to take to gather qualitative data are all part of this strategy of research methods. Consider research methodology as the glue that binds together all these research methods with your theoretical framework.

Writing about research design involves you writing about the plan of attack you employed for your study. This is your chance to tell your readers directly how you actually planned and conducted your study. Avoid delivering a lesson on the topic of your choice of methods and design, rather describe the mechanics of how you are using and applying particular methods specifically in your study. Explain how you understand your research design and cite your methods. Cite the authors whose methods you use in a way that supports *your* work, rather than their work.

Your writing needs to show how you are employing specific research methods by sharing the reasons for your choice of a particular framework design. Every qualitative study is unique, and as such, requires the use of specialized methods which are most appropriate for that inquiry. Share your thinking behind your decision making especially given the flexible emergent design challenges qualitative researchers experience. Be transparent and show your audience how your decisions strengthen the overall quality of your study. Remember that throughout this dynamic process the focus of your study does not change.

It is a great idea to use your ethics/human subjects' protection application as a writing aid to identify steps you have taken in the methods section of your study. This can help you show others how you connect your research focus to your research questions and your data. Further, it is important to expect the unexpected as your research unfolds. Qualitative research is flexible, emergent and fraught with ambiguity (Denzin & Lincoln, 2018; Maxwell, 2013; Patton, 2015). As a result, your presentation of your study methods requires ongoing adjustments to any number of aspects to the inquiry. These decision moments can involve the types of data available, the data analysis methods chosen and other elements of your study design. Anticipating a need to be flexible and making thoughtful adjustments, with clear rationale, allows the researcher to comfortably address such events in a credible transparent manner.

5.A PRESENTING RESEARCH DESIGN THROUGH WRITING

Your success in writing about your research is dependent upon how clearly you articulate the central focus of your study. A helpful writing tip is to save all versions of this statement as you brainstorm, edit, and refine for clarity and alignment to your study design. Once you have the focus statement clearly written in one or two sentences, consider it written in stone. Do not change or edit this statement further. This research focus represents the heart of your study and is central to your story arc. As you continue to write, keep your focus consistently connected to every aspect of the study. Your study focus will provide the framework (boundaries) for everything you do as you progress your research.

> A **helpful tip** is to print out your focus statement when it is finalized and keep it close. Perhaps you might like to tape it to your monitor or to the front of your research folder. Find a prominent place, display it and keep your focus statement front and center at all times.

5.A.1 Linking to Theory

Determining your theoretical approach to a qualitative study is a research design decision which must be considered thoughtfully in the early stages of planning. This process is not simply something a researcher does by either falling back to their favorite approach with which they have grown comfortable, nor is it a process of randomly picking a theory off the shelf. Rather, the process requires due diligence in identifying which qualitative theoretical orientation best supports a specific inquiry by addressing the focus of the study and aligning with the study purpose.

Wolcott (2001a) discussed this nagging question of how best to go about determining a theoretical approach by suggesting that you view your use of theory as a means to help clarify your research purpose which tells your audience what you are up to in your study. This clarification will benefit both you, the researcher, as well as your intended audience (p. 189). The following is provided by Wolcott particularly for those qualitative researchers who are somewhat unsure about the theoretical orientation of their study:

> For those not initially attracted to or comfortable with theory in the first place, nagging issues of what-to-do-about-theory never get answered to everyone's satisfaction and never go away. The essential thing is to learn how to deal with them in a professionally adequate manner to ensure either that theory serves to guide and clarify (rather than to intimate), or that the orienting function that theory addresses is accomplished even in the absence of theory made explicit (pp. 183–184).

The important point here is to (yet again) find a way that works for you in drawing qualitative theoretical insights that advance your writing. It is not the intent of this text to present detailed discussions into qualitative theories. There are a wide range of excellent texts available to further explore this fascinating area of qualitative research. The following list offers a few recommendations for your reference:

Anfara Jr., V. A., & Mertz, N. T. (2014). *Theoretical frameworks in qualitative research*.
Charmaz, K. (2014). *Constructing grounded theory* (2nd ed.).

Corbin, J., & Strauss, A. (2015). *Basics of qualitative research* (4th ed.).
Denzin, N. K. & Lincoln, Y. S. (Eds.). (2018). *Introduction: The discipline and practice of qualitative research* (pp. 1–26), In N. K. Denzin & Y. S. Lincoln (Eds.), *The Sage handbook of qualitative research* (5th ed.).
Gibson, W., & Brown, A. (2009). Theory, grounded theory and analysis. In W. Gibson & A. Brown, *Working with qualitative data* (pp. 15–32).
Hughes, S. A., & Pennington, J. L. (2017). *Autoethnography*.
O'Reilly, M., & Kiyimba, N. (2015). *Advanced qualitative research: A guide to using theory*.
Patton, M. Q. (2015). Making methods decisions. In M. Q. Patton, *Qualitative research & evaluation methods* (4th ed., pp. 85–168).
Schwandt, T. A. (2015). *Dictionary of qualitative inquiry* (4th ed.).
Youngblood Jackson, A., & Mazzei, L. (2011). *Thinking with theory in qualitative research: Viewing data across multiple perspectives*.

If you are a novice researcher with limited exposure to literature on qualitative theory, then you may want to begin by reading Chapter 3 (pp. 85–168) in the Patton (2015) text. Although the Patton reading is comprehensive, do not consider this as inclusive of all qualitative theoretical perspectives. Once you identify a potential theoretical orientation of interest for your study then refer to Schwandt (2015) and use this dictionary to identify additional related literature to review on the theory of your choice. By exploring a range of literature on your choice of qualitative theory you will deepen your understanding and strengthen the overall quality of your writing.

5.A.2 Connecting Research Focus and Research Questions

Connecting your writing to theory is a good first step but is not considered sufficient in clearly presenting the framework of the overall study research design. To tell a strong story, you need to connect your writing around the focus and show how the focus links to the central research question. A qualitative thesis or dissertation represents in depth scholarly work into original social science research. Regardless if you are working on a dissertation or a scholarly journal article, your design must connect the focus with the questions your work seeks to answer. You are the researcher driving the inquiry and through your writing you are sharing this journey with your readers. Your journey is a story arc which is held together with a clear focus. Chasing side stories and interesting but distracting diversionary paths may seem appealing but will confuse and weaken your message. Your study raises key research questions about this focus. It is your responsibility to connect the reader to these questions and ultimately provide credible answers to what you found.

Figure 5.1 shows the interconnectedness between focus, data and questions while the question mark is asking you to show how they all connect. Think about how you can make this thinking visible to your readers. How can you further clarify the meaning of the question mark for your readers? What is particularly important? Where and when does it matter?

5.A.3 Strategies to Align Your Research Questions and Research Focus

This chapter has covered a lot of ground by connecting theory to your research focus and research questions, as well as connecting to methods and then to data. Here are a few things to remember:

1. Specific language has different meanings for different disciplines. Make your work accessible to others by minimizing the use of jargon and discipline-specific language; for example, if you are using acronyms in your work, make sure that you define them to a broader audience.

2. Key terms in the area of your research are an important part of your writing. As you delve deeper into your research, you become very familiar with these terms, others not so much. Make sure that all your key terms are clearly defined and listed in a Glossary. For example, in a dissertation, this list may be presented in Chapter 1 or in an Appendix.

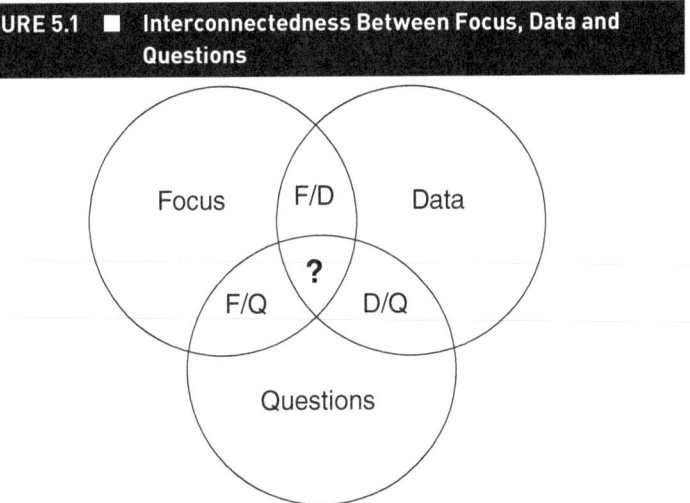

FIGURE 5.1 ■ Interconnectedness Between Focus, Data and Questions

3. Find ways to show your audience how you are making these connections. One example of this is shown in Table 5.1. This table is an illustration of a type of table you can present in your writing showing the connections between the data and research questions. This particular table visually demonstrates your research design by showing your reader how you have made connections between your research questions and your data sources.

5.B BUILDING YOUR RESEARCH ARGUMENT

A common criticism raised by academic editors, reviewers, and external examiners is mentioned when authors fail to present a cohesive argument or don't present the argument early and clearly (Belcher, 2019, Olson, 1997). As the writer, it is your job to make these connections clearly and succinctly early in

TABLE 5.1 ■ Connecting Data and Research Questions

Data Types	Data Sources	Alignment to Research Questions
Interviews	P1, P2, FG1	Interview questions 1–5 are related to research question 3
Observations	Stock Exchange	These observations are related to research question 4
	Boardroom	These observations are related to research question 5
	Planning Meetings	These observations are related to research question 6
Documents	Legislation	Evidence supporting social policy reform
	Annual Reports	Evidence supporting the study focus
	Company Website	Vision and mission, products, services
Memos	M1-8	Audit trail of emergent design
	A1-12	Findings and interpretation of multiple meanings
	R1-6	Researcher as Instrument

[P = participant; FG = focus group; M = methods; A = analytic; R = reflections]

Source: Adapted from Kaczynski, Salmona, & Smith (2014). Reproduced with permission.

your writing. To help your audience grasp your qualitative argument, spend some time early on clarifying your research purpose statement. Refer back to Section 1.B for a discussion and resources for writing the research study focus and purpose statements and Section 4.C, for an example. The purpose statement provides the starting point for you to develop and strengthen your argument for studying a particular social problem. Make sure your audience knows what you are thinking and from where your path of reasoning emerges.

An essential starting point when building your qualitative argument is to remind yourself what the social problem is that your study set out to address. Your writing will provide a well-defined path showing what it is you seek to know about this problem. To do this, ask yourself if you have correctly identified and documented what the actual social problem is that your study addresses. Jacobs (2011) emphasizes the importance of giving attention to a well-framed problem statement when you are presenting your argument to others with the following comment:

> Research problems do not exist in nature just waiting to be plucked out by some observant researcher. Instead, they are artificial entities that come together only through the intense efforts of the researcher. (p. 127)

When writing about the social problem you will need to identify which issues you intend to examine related to the broad topic of interest. This is more than a narrowing of a topic, rather it requires you to reveal a gap to a troubling or perplexing situation. Your study is unique in that you have chosen particular aspects to a social problem and your study design aims to draw upon your choice of evidence to support your argument.

With the problem in mind, review how you initially decided on your approach. This train of thought can help you determine the essence of what you are studying. The important point here is that you can clearly express your research focus statement. As discussed earlier, the focus statement is a carefully crafted sentence that expresses what your study is about and defines the parameters of your qualitative argument. If you are having difficulty succinctly expressing your focus statement, you may find it helpful to try the following activity. Express your focus statement by beginning with an exploratory verb that best represents your desired approach (Creswell, 2009, p. 130–131):

- seek to **better understand** . . .
- **investigate** events involving . . .
- **discover** new insights into . . .
- **explore** a specific instance . . .

- **describe** the experience of . . .
- **tell** the story of or about . . .

You need to decide which of these qualitative exploratory verbs best frames your research design into a complex social problem. Pick one of these paths to begin building your argument.

An argument is something that is woven throughout your research study from start to finish. Each point in your argument is positioned like a stepping stone which you are placing for your reader to guide them across a stream. The intent of your argument is to credibly present the evidence of your research to inform, persuade, influence, and possibly promote social change. A qualitative argument draws upon recognized social science research practices such as the literature review, data triangulation, data gathering, data analysis, and conclusions which are woven together into a compelling story. Staying inductive in the early stages of your study is an important qualitative practice, as your weave this argument. Avoid jumping to a solution or promoting an approach how the social problem can be resolved. By staying flexible and open to diverse points of view your argument will be more credible and can generate unique insights. Try looking at the problem as a multifaceted prism with each facet a unique window from which to see the problem from a different angle. This inductive approach promotes the discovery of richer deeper meanings from the analysis of data.

Using your qualitative theoretical orientation to guide and clarify your writing will further aid in building a credible argument. The theoretical perspective upon which you draw for your study will shape and define your qualitative inquiry approach. This can be seen through the researcher voice you employ and how you present the voice of the participants through your writing. What a participant says in an interview and how they behave in a social setting may be contradictory and stand apart even further from how they express their views in private. This does not necessarily mean that the participant lied or that misrepresentation occurred. More likely, there is more going on than what the researcher saw or heard. These complex routine social interactions were explored by the sociologist Erving Goffman (deRoche & deRoche, 2010) during the 1950s when he first introduced the concepts of front stage and backstage. In essence, social behaviors are performed on stages such as at a restaurant when the waiter behaves at the customers table differently than how the waiter behaves in the kitchen behind a closed door. Your argument thus can use theory to explore social interactions with an inductive openness which you employ to unravel complex and potentially conflicting evidence.

As mentioned previously, when building a qualitative argument begin with the focus statement of your study. Moving forward with the argument involves staying connected to the focus as you explore related literature and gather qualitative data. It is important throughout that both the literature and the qualitative data are used to support the argument. As the researcher, it is your responsibility to avoid allowing either the literature or the qualitative data to overshadow the argument. If you sense that the argument is getting lost in the story, then you may need to refine or expand your use of literature. Referring back to your literature concept map may be a helpful way to identify areas in your argument that need further attention. The other possibility is that your reporting of qualitative data may require further analysis. Remember that in either case, you are using the literature and findings as evidence to support the argument.

5.C DIFFERENT VOICES IN WRITING

As you continue to develop your writing voice, consider the different types of writing voices which other qualitative researchers have adopted in their work. Researchers' writing voices will vary considerably given the unique differences with research focus, purpose of the study, theoretical orientation, data sources, and intended target audience in each study. When deciding on your approach to your writing voice think about "who you are" in your writing with particular attention to how you intend to critically speak to diversity and diverse representations. Diversity in writing, and writer voice, has been vital to the growth of critical work in qualitative research.

Take a moment and acknowledge that there is no one "correct" approach to writing, whether it be writing voice, style, or how you present your findings. Critical scholarship has long critiqued Eurocentric methodologies that reinforce this misnomer (Patel, 2016; Wemigwase & Tuck, 2019; Zuberi & Bonilla-Silva, 2008). Below are two excerpts from scholars who used critical paradigms to guide their methodology. As these examples show, theory and methodology can directly inform writing voice (reflexive, active, confessional) and data presentation.

 Consider the following two examples and note the different voices being used in each example. Use these examples to further develop the identification of your own voice in your work. Then try to write a short memo in your own voice about your work. As you review your draft try to gauge if you are starting to capture your authentic voice. You may find it helpful to share your draft with a new reader for further critical feedback.

VOICES IN WRITING, EXAMPLE 1

Bold. Brown. Brains. Solange's lyrics forever reminds me that despite how unwelcomed or estranged I am made to feel in this academic space this is my 46 Tales from the Ivory Tower home— 'tis where I belong. Because within the vastness of Colorblanco's whiteness, exists an academy whose stereotypical characterizations of me sadly defines them more so than it does me. Refusing to feel like a forever foreigner (Park, 2011) inside my own academic home and refusing to withstand their vitriol, rage, and vehemence when I don't perform submissiveness, docility, and servility I stand. Appalled and, at the same time, threatened that I am bold enough to assert my humanity and expertise—while they attempt to control my body, mind, and spirit with their racialization and sexualization of me—I again stand. I stand tall—all five feet of me—realizing that their awe of how unapologetic I am is a stereotypical presumption that women of color should be apologetic for asserting themselves. In the end this is not my issue. Rather, this is their issue with me being at home with the boldness, Brownness, and beautifulness of my mind, body, and soul. Instead of identifying, realizing, let alone be cognizant enough to welcome it, their vitriolic projections becomes a sad display of their own white insecurities. Even amidst that, I stand.

(Matias, Walker, & del Hierro, 2019, pp. 45–46. Reproduced with permission.)

In this first example, the writer offers insight into their work using critical autoethnography as their theoretical orientation. A confessional and reflexive active voice is adopted, emphasizing social location in relation to structure and disrupting dominant narratives.

VOICES IN WRITING, EXAMPLE 2

I had recently read some of those issues myself and smiled at the way in which Esperanza had extended the LatCrits' work to fit within her developing framework in education. I added, "Robert Chang's (1993) work also reminds would-be-progressives that racism raises its ugly head in communities of varying skin tones, accents, cultures, and immigration status."

Esperanza pulled out a wrinkled newsletter from her backpack and read a highlighted section. "Check out this quote from a UCLA Chicano Professor: 'In Los Angeles as in the nation, such social issues as poverty, welfare, affirmative action, crime, and immigration have a racial face. These issues have a color and the color is usually black, brown, red, or yellow.' Our experiences are racialized both inside and outside the classroom."

I responded, "The racial faces of Communities of Color differ state-by-state, district-by-district, yet have a history of commonality in regards to experiences with structural inequality both inside and outside schools."

Esperanza stirred the whipped cream into her coffee as she took in what I just said. She continued to speak a few seconds later. "As the only Chicana in my PhD cohort, in the beginning of the program I would often raise issues concerning the implications of policy for Chicana/o students only to have my comments given a nod of courtesy critical race and Lat crit theory and method 479 before the subject was dismissed and attention directed elsewhere. After a while, I just stopped participating. Then I'd feel even worse, like my silence makes me complicit with the ignorance of the professors and students who claim to be social justice educators but who are blind to the ways in which they themselves 'do school'."

"What do you mean by 'do school'?" I asked.

"I mean we sort and stratify students according to racial, gender, and socioeconomic attributes. We create a meritocracy, which assumes all students begin on a level playing field. We develop a hierarchy of relationships between professors and students, the researcher and the researched, the academy and the community," Esperanza replied.

(Critical race and LatCrit theory and method: Counter-storytelling, in D. G. Solorzano & T. J. Yosso, *International Journal of Qualitative Studies in Education* 14(4), 2001, Routledge. Reprinted by permission of Taylor & Francis Ltd., http://www.tandfonline.com).

In this second example, the writer offers insight into their work using critical race theory counter-stories as their theoretical orientation. An active voice is also adopted, emphasizing social location in relation to structure and disrupting dominant narratives.

****

Take a moment to consider who you are and what you bring to your work. With this in mind, approach your writing knowing what voice you intend to use. The positioning of the researcher's voice can serve different roles: someone sharing the excitement of a new discovery, a detective seeking clues to unravel a mystery, a teacher presenting lessons learned, or an auto ethnographer self-exploring. Your task here is to discover your voice in this research and how you wish to express yourself in your work.

The following are suggested readings for further information into the issues of researcher voice:

Denzin, N. K. & Lincoln, Y. S. (Ed.). (2018). *The SAGE handbook of qualitative research* (5th ed.). SAGE. **[Feminist Voices, p. 160]**

Marshall, C., Rossman, G. B., & Blanco, G. L. (2021). *Designing qualitative research* (7th ed.). *SAGE.* **[Identity-Based Forms of Oppression, p. 36]**

Patton, M. Q. (2015). *Qualitative research & evaluation methods* (4th ed.). SAGE. **[Voice Is More Than Grammar, pp. 73–74]**

Wolcott, H. F. (2009). *Writing up qualitative research* (3rd ed.). SAGE. **[Your Story and Voice, pp. 16–17]**

<u>Remember</u>: Strong writing can also include diverse methodologies as different ways of writing. Examples of diverse writing styles that reflect our contemporary landscape might include narrative, indigenous, or feminist methodologies. Finding your own "voice" and writing up qualitative research could include images, aspects of graphic novel, collage and many other forms of expression. Challenge yourself to be creative as you look for your own voice.

Chapter 5 gave you a lot to think about as you are starting to write your research design in a form that is accessible to the reader. Chapter 6 now moves you from thinking about your research design and your use of voice to thinking about managing, and writing about, your data.

6 WRITING ABOUT DATA

Now that you are well into writing up your work, it is time to consider how best to ensure that your work is supported with strong evidence. Sharing your findings with your intended audience involves drawing upon this evidence in a convincing way. Remember, it is important in your writing to engage the reader and keep them interested in your story. Your audience wants to know what you found from your research study. Research findings are how you present and share this message. Findings are drawn from your analysis of data and are informed by the literature which you have chosen to frame this inquiry. Throughout your analysis you will have been writing memos and creating visuals of your developing findings. Now it is your task to refine the story arc and share your data in a way that allows the audience to better understand your research process which you are using to draw outcomes and present conclusions.

6.A USING DATA TO BUILD CONNECTIONS

As you turn your attention to your data, it is very important to keep in mind that this is where the main thrust of analysis work begins. Previous chapters have discussed writing up the introduction, research design, and theoretical underpinnings which are all critical elements to framing your story. All writing to this point has been developed so that it has meaning to its intended audience. However, your work with data represents the concrete evidence upon which you will build the foundation to your findings. Data, and how you communicate their appropriateness, the way they were gathered, from whom they were gathered, how they were organized and used, and the ways in which they can be analyzed and presented is what separates findings established via empirical studies from stories based on anecdotes and narrow, subjective perspectives. In essence, your data must be an integral part of the writing process and the story of your research.

6.A.1 WHAT ARE DATA?

This is an important question for anyone engaging in the research process, as the answer will help to identify and clarify what you are looking for, what information you seek, what forms the data take, and how you will use these data to strengthen your research story and arguments.

From a social science research perspective, data, in general, can be thought of as pieces of information that can be defined based on their source, their form, and their utility in how they can be used to organize, analyze, transform, and represent the goals of a research project. These data can come from others (or other places), oneself, historical records and artifacts, groups, public sources, and online. They can be descriptive numbers, words, images, video, or audio. They can be structured or unstructured, newly created or gathered or existing, digital or analogue and, most importantly, useful or not for a researcher's intended goals. Data gathering can sometimes be overwhelming in this age of endless available sources and types of data. Coming up with the most appropriate answer to the question of what data you want and need is challenging.

A helpful strategy for gathering appropriate data is to try thinking about your project in this way: What are you hoping to argue? Who do you wish will hear your story? What will be the most useful data to support your arguments and present them in a way that the intended consumers of your research will find the most valuable? Furthermore, reflect on your resources in terms of time, funding, skills, participants and colleagues, as you consider what data you can realistically afford to gather, process, analyze, and present without running out of time, money, or sanity.

At this stage of your writing, you will have identified a diverse range of data out there and available to you. You have created a written focus statement of your study and are now determining what type of data may be helpful in answering your research questions. Further, you have thought about the kinds of evidence that will be most convincing to the variety of members in your intended audience. This is unlikely to be a homogenous group, and presenting a consistent thesis grounded in the data will help assure that your work will be engaging and valuable to the range of consumers in your target audience. You have also thought about how much time and money you have available to support you in data gathering endeavors. Now think about strengthening your study by drawing on the ideas represented in Figure 6.1 (Kaczynski et al., 2014) as a guide for finding and adding credible evidence from multiple data sources.

FIGURE 6.1 ■ Finding Credible Evidence From Multiple Data Sources

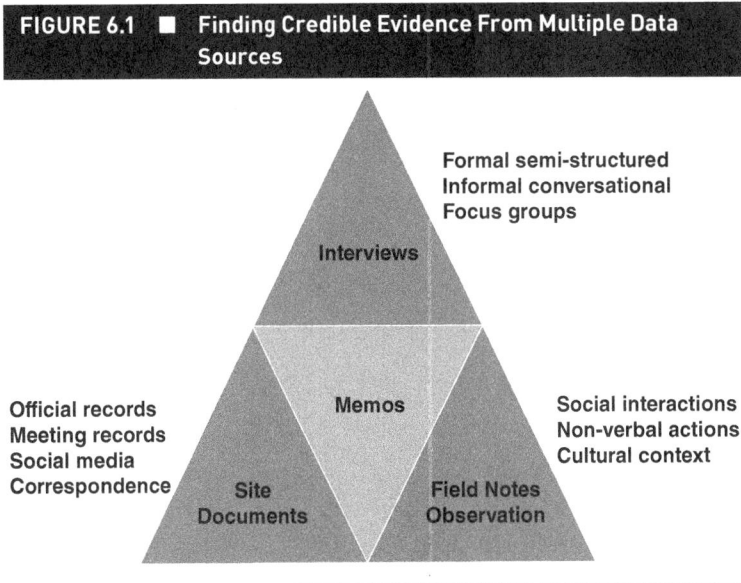

Source: Adapted from Kaczynski, Salmona, & Smith (2014). Reproduced with permission.

As you challenge yourself to consider what data you are going to use in your research, think about how many data you can gather from one event such as an interview. The following list, in Table 6.1, serves to illustrate a few of the different types of data that you can gather associated with each or all of your interviews.

6.A.2 Sorting and Organizing Data

Qualitative data is gathered to describe rather than measure, the attributes, characteristics or properties of something. Mostly, this type of data is collected from interviews, field note observations, diaries, documents, as well as maps, photographs, and other printed materials. Your data are a resource that needs to be well-organized, to be as useful as possible. Always ensure that all your data are accurate, for example, review your interview transcripts to ensure verbatim correctness and precision. Then give attention to organizing your data.

Step 1 is to find a way to group and categorize your data. Earlier in this book (Section 3.C.1) version control and important steps to take in saving everything you write and create was discussed. Here the emphasis is on identifying your data carefully, as this is the key to any system you might use to sort and organize your data. Data management also enhances the tracking of all your data, from fieldwork to analysis. This tracking system will contain details of individuals, dates, and sites including all sources and context.

TABLE 6.1 ■ Different Types of Data for Interviews

Examples of Different Types of Data Associated Interviews

Memos: four types—Methods, Reflective, Analytic, Inductive–Deductive Shifts
Transcripts
Demographic data about participants
Translation
Observer comments/notes to self/annotations
Field observations—during interview
Field notes—interview site (setting)
Site documents, for example, organizational website/mission statements/policy documents
Interview artifacts, for example, drawing how they see the organization
Photographs/Photo journaling
Diagrams of interview site
Predata, Postdata
Email chains—correspondence before/during/after
Participant journals/memos/diaries/reflections
Member checks

Source: Adapted from Salmona, Lieber, & Kaczynski (2020, p. 65). Reproduced with permission.

Organize your data by category or topic; name your data with descriptive names; use README files throughout your work to explain your data organization and context; backup often with multiple copies (use secure cloud storage, external and internal hard drives, USBs). Make sure that you always store any backup in accordance with the conditions of your ethics or IRB approval.

Some of your data may not be electronic data, for example, arts-based collections, diaries, old photos, historical documents, and physical artifacts. These data must still be organized and categorized using filing systems, filing cabinets, and index files. Categorizing these types of artifacts electronically has the advantage of enabling the index system to be added to your online data tracking system (see Section 6.A.4, Use Digital Tools to Manage More Data, for more on this).

Now you need to develop procedures about formatting all your data. For example, if you find something useful on the internet, consider copying the HTML text, and then pasting as text into a Word document. This will remove any tricky formatting and make data analysis an easier and cleaner process. Take some time to anonymize your data, so that others can work with you through your analysis without risking any ethical breaches.

Most importantly, have a plan of action with a realistic timeline. Work on this plan regularly and systematically. Organized data will be readily accessible and high-quality data management will help you preserve the integrity of your data after you have completed your research.

6.A.3 Use Digital Tools to Find More Data

Using digital tools in your research can allow you to think more creatively about what data you can gather and what data you can analyze. Stimulating yourself to find more data can strengthen your study and allow you to investigate the social problem at a deeper level. Always come back to your research focus statement and research questions and be clear how your data connects back to these constructs. A wide variety of data will also strengthen your story line as your research takes form.

Richards (2021) discusses different ways of making (collecting and gathering) data by clarifying your study design. She reminds us to avoid relying on one type of data such as interviews. Rather, extend your world view and challenge yourself to find many different types of data. "In an everyday situation we would use several ways of finding out and learning" (p. 59). All research projects can be strengthened by viewing the topic under investigation in multiple ways. Digital tools allow you to broaden your horizons and think creatively about data gathering, management and analysis. Remember that this amazing amount of available data in digital and public domain forms may not always be reliable data. Nonetheless, really challenge yourself to be brave and investigate the potential qualitative data stored and communicated digitally.

Digital records do not need to be transcribed and are readily available for analysis when they are retrieved in digital form. As you are working with these records, spend some time thinking about how you want to manage and save these digital records. One way is to make a PDF of the digital record; another is to copy the content and paste it as text into a Word document. This removes any formatting in the digital record and leaves you with only the text, which can make future analysis easier.

You can find data from websites, listservs, blogs, publicly available documents, online survey tools, social media, images, and transcription tools and you can build data interactively through online tools such as Google Docs and Google Forms—subject to any ethics approvals. "New innovations offer new data sources such as Web pages, tweets, or geo-location data captured through GPS devices" (Gilbert et al., 2014, p. 222).

In any data gathering plan, consistency and a systematic approach are very important. A systemic approach to data gathering allows you to show how you are building those connections in your data; and consistency in data gathering strategies will help you to manage your data well (see next Section 6.A.4 for more on managing your data).

> As a qualitative fieldwork reminder, stay open to triangulating and gathering more data as you continue to construct meanings. Qualitative studies never really end, you just eventually run out of time. As Wolcott (2001a) said, "our works are never completed . . . what we really do is abandon them" (p. 35).

How might a researcher gather data using digital tools?

- You can locate and download data from an endless range of websites, some of which might require fees or membership. However, globally more and more data are being digitized for long-term maintenance, availability, and protection. An example of this growing trend may be seen at the Qualitative Data Repository (n.d.) hosted by the Center for Qualitative and Multi-Method Inquiry, a unit of the Maxwell School of Citizenship and Public Affairs at Syracuse University.

- Using a camera, digital video, or audio recorder can enhance the gathering of valuable data for your fieldwork. The growing popularity of digital video features in smart phones, iPads, and other devices makes this type of data gathering increasingly convenient.

- Participant-led video diaries, online participant videos, and video-based observations are a few examples of the growing popularity of digital innovations.

- Web scraping is another strategy to gather digital data. Remember to be careful what sources you target in terms of legal and privacy issues. See Chapter 7 Obtaining Data from the Web Using Python (Kaefer & Kaefer, 2020) for more on this.

- Social media and chat room data is yet another source of digital data. Maybe you have a huge following on Twitter or Facebook (or know someone who does). It may surprise you how freely people will respond to a call out for feedback.

- Ask people to provide information via forms, surveys, texting, verbal messaging. There are many digital tools to help gather these data with features to contact people and provide them with some format to share their information. These digital tools also provide you with the ability to store and organize the data provided to you. A few examples for you to consider are: listservs, websites, and survey tools such as SurveyMonkey, SurveyGizmo, and Qualtrics. Google Forms is another simple and easy way to gather data online as can be seen in Figures 6.2 and 6.3 below.

6.A.3.1 Google Forms:

Google Forms is an example of an easy to create internet-based form designed to gather data. When you create the form, which can be edited at any time, you have options of multiple choice, short- or long-text answers, or numeric answer within a range. This allows the researcher to collect demographic data as well as rich text-based answers. Figure 6.2 shows an example of a Google

FIGURE 6.2 ■ Example of Google Form Set up for Data Gathering

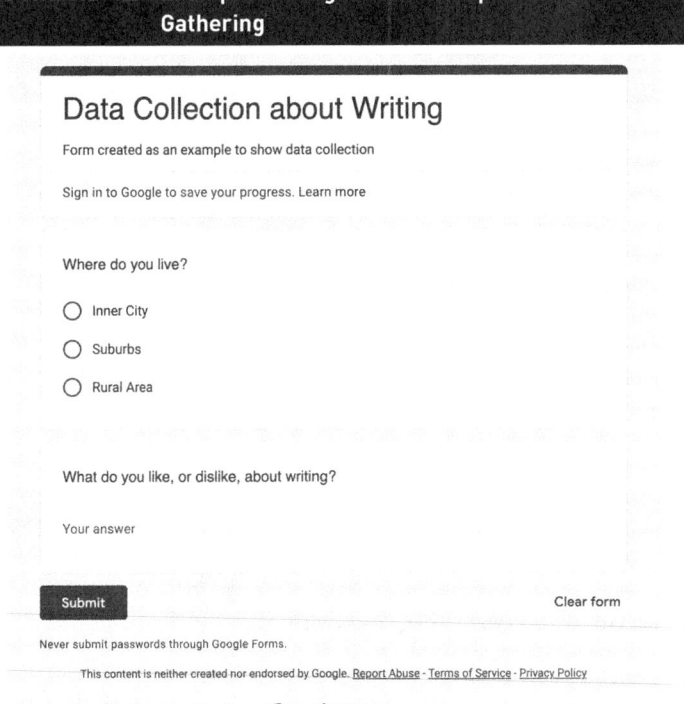

Google Forms

Form prepared as an example showing a multiple-choice question, together with a short answer question.

Once you have prepared your Google Form, you can immediately begin data gathering by sharing a link with your participants. Figure 6.3 shows how the summary results can be tabulated and presented in Google Forms.

Table 6.2 shows how this same data can be exported into a spreadsheet for easy access to the text to incorporate into your analysis.

FIGURE 6.3 ■ Example of Google Form Response

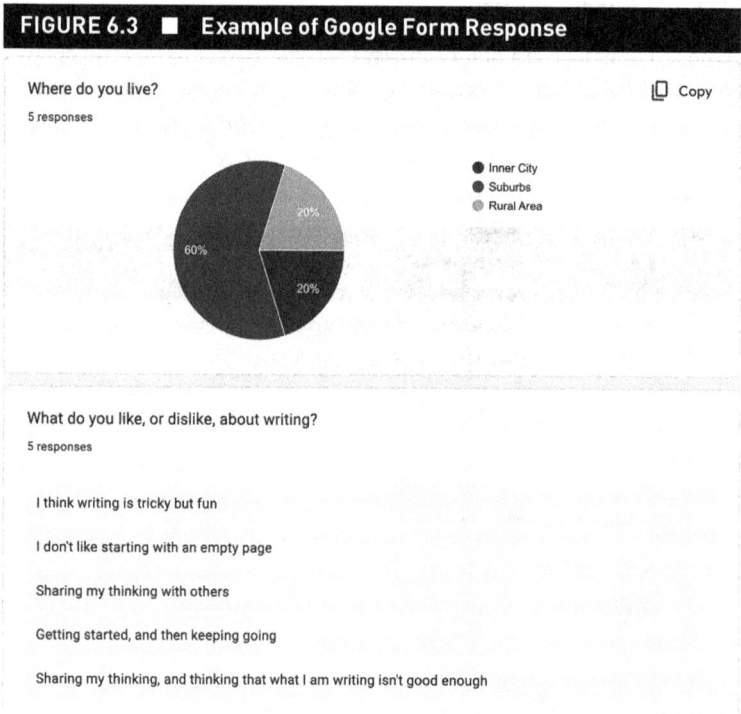

TABLE 6.2 ■ Example of Data Export for Google Forms

What do you like, or dislike, about writing?	
Inner City	I think writing is tricky but fun
Suburbs	I don't like starting with an empty page
Rural Area	Sharing my thinking with others
Suburbs	Getting started, and then keeping going
Suburbs	Sharing my thinking, and thinking that what I am writing isn't good enough

6.A.4 Use Digital Tools to Manage More Data

Data management can be defined as "a system for organizing, cataloging, and indexing these materials in the data log that makes it possible to retrieve them efficiently, duplicate them, and use them for different tasks. The system you design will, in turn, affect the way one conceptualizes the process of analyzing the data" (Schwandt, 2015, p. 67). In other words, it is simply an organizational process in which digital tools can help you make this process more efficient and allow you to manage more data than you might without such tools.

A strong data management plan will outline how a researcher will handle their data both during the research and once the research is complete. This is likely part of the original ethics application for the research as well. Thorough management of data includes strategies for data collection, documentation, processing, analysis, and storage for the lifetime of the research. A good overview of issues related to the managing and sharing of research data is provided by Corti et al. (2014).

There are reasons why it is important to pay attention to data management: (1) to provide systematic access during the analysis process, (2) to protect your data, and (3) enable your data to be used again. The data may be useful to you in a follow-up study, or may be stored as anonymized data in a trusted digital data repository for use by others. In a robust qualitative research study, a researcher will collect data from many different sources which must be managed in a systematic, ethical, and transparent way. Table 6.3 gives some examples of different types of data and how they may be stored.

Here are some questions you might ask yourself to see whether you are managing your data well:

TABLE 6.3 ■ Storage for Different Types of Data

Examples of Storage for Different Types of Data

Interviews	Stored as digital audio .mp3 files and transcripts in MS Word
Public Data	Electronic archives, news items stored in Excel
Social Media	Exported and stored in Excel
Images	Stored as digital files such as .jpeg, .png
Survey Results	Exported and stored in Excel

- Can you find all your consent forms for all of your data?
- Where are all your data stored? Are they all secure and backed up appropriately?
- How many interviews have you completed?
- What other data have you gathered? Can you list and describe all your data?
- Are your file names clear and easy to understand?

You can organize your data in either a process way or an analytical way. You can group your data by its type, source, date or any other data characteristic. Any organization or management of your data will include connecting data that are related to other data in some way. Connections can be built through names, memos, links, or codes and these connections or groupings may be thematic, theory driven, or data driven (Gilbert et al, 2014, p. 224).

6.A.4.1 Steps to Good Data Management

- Avoid chaos in your data. Establish a realistic timeline, so that you can always give yourself enough time to manage your data well and avoid rushed work.
- Organize your data files by topic, type, or date range—whatever makes the best sense to you.
- Put a README file in every folder to explain and describe the files stored in the folder and any context needed to understand the organization.
- Choose and follow a clear descriptive file naming convention which is essential for good data management (this was discussed earlier in Section 3.C.1). Always print the file name as a footer in all your research documents, so that you always know in which version you are working. The file name may include data type, data collection site, date of data collection, or anything else that is meaningful to you in your research.
- Develop a data-tracking system.
- Make sure you have consistency in all your documents. Establish and document transcription and translation procedures. For example, create a template for any transcription work, so that all the

transcribed files follow the same format. Remember to transcribe verbatim and think about what types of information in your data need protection. Always give attention to protecting participant confidentiality.

- Back up often. Keep at least three copies of your data in at least two locations. For example, keep one copy on a secure server and one hard copy of your complete data set secured in a locked drawer. Consider using secure cloud storage, a backup drive or your own computer. Consider security and availability. For example, it is a great idea to remove all sensitive information (anonymize) before storing your data.

When considering the different ways which digital tools may be used to manage data, you will first have to decide that you want to use a digital tool to manage your data, then you must decide which tool you want to use. These are two very important considerations which help determine how you archive and analyze your data. First and foremost, a digital tool is only a tool. As mentioned in Chapter 3, you are the craftsperson; how you employ such tools and control their use is entirely up to you (Salmona & Kaczynski, 2016). As you make these decisions, maintain a fundamental perspective on what you will want to do with your data in the future.

Blismas and Dainty (2003) raised an important issue in their discussion about the use of technology to manage, and analyze, qualitative data:

All quality research should be preceded with a comprehensive examination of the possible methods and methodologies available for the research question, followed by justification for the choice made. Inherent within such an approach is an understanding of the logic and mechanisms of the various methodologies, as well as an appreciation of their intrinsic strengths and weaknesses. CAQDAS in no way alleviates the need for this process. In fact, it puts greater onus on the researcher to understand the mechanisms of the software and actively develop strategies to counteract these weaknesses. (p. 457)

When choosing which technology, if any, you will use in your research, consider reviewing the resources at the Computer Assisted Qualitative Data Analysis Networking Project (CAQDAS Networking Project, n.d.). The CAQDAS Networking Project provides training and information in the use of a range of digital tools and applications designed to assist in the analysis of qualitative data.

As you are choosing which technology, if any, you will use to manage your data, you will also be writing memos about how you made your choice. This is very important as you must discuss this in your writing.

- Why did you choose to use a digital tool for your research?
- Which digital tool did you decide to use?
- How did you come to this decision?

Organizing and managing your data is an important part of the process in any qualitative research. A strong approach will help you manage the large amounts of unstructured data you generate in your study. This is something you will keep coming back to as you collect more data and develop more ideas about your data (Gilbert et al., 2014; Paulus et al., 2013). Remember as you go through the process, it is very important to write, write, write!

- Write design memos about how you manage your data.
- Write researcher reflective memos capturing your developing thinking about how you see yourself in the process.
- Write analytic memos as you begin to build connections in your data.

As discussed earlier in Section 1.B, all of this memo writing can end up as data and some extracts from your memos may well end up in the final writing piece for your project. Also, by engaging in consistent memo writing, you will improve the overall quality and productivity of your writing.

Gathering and working with the many forms of data and employing strategies to manage this foundation to your research evidence, raises an important consideration of description before interpretation. It is always important to carefully separate description from interpretation (Patton, 2015, p. 534). Although it is tempting to interpret before describing, description always comes first, as data interpretation represents qualitative meaning making which is analysis. Before you move your writing into an analysis phase you need to carefully separate your descriptive writing from analytic interpretation. This next section explores how you may approach this task.

6.B BUILDING STRONG DATA: THICK DESCRIPTION

As mentioned at the beginning of this chapter, credible writing draws upon strong evidence that is well organized and accessible. Sharing your work with your intended audience involves drawing upon this evidence in a convincing way. As you proceed with your writing you will begin to discover interesting insights into your research. Findings are drawn from these insights and interpretation of meanings in your data. Shank (2002) explains "the most basic form of interpretation is description" (p.74). Describing events, people, behavior, and social interactions involves the researcher gathering and interpreting data. How well you describe this type of qualitative data shapes the quality and clarity of the meanings you draw from your research.

To improve your descriptive writing consider carefully what is involved. The term *thick description* was introduced to the field of qualitative research by Geertz (1973, p. 6) as a means to move beyond thin evidence by presenting thicker, more compelling, empirical evidence. Thicker is a more nuanced description of social actions and interactions that captures physical behaviors together with their context so that they can be better understood by outsiders.

The definition of the term, *thick description*, has evolved over time as the field of qualitative research increasingly adopted the concept. In 1989, Denzin described thick description as doing, "more than record what a person is doing. It goes beyond mere fact and surface appearances. It presents detail, context, emotion, and the webs of social relationships that join persons to one another" (p. 83). In 2001, this thinking further developed with a broader definition that embraces more characteristics about the social context. Schwandt (2015) describes this as, "not simply a matter of amassing relevant detail. Rather to thickly describe social action is actually to begin to interpret it by recording the circumstances, meanings, intentions, strategies, motivations, and so on that characterize a particular episode. It is this interpretive characteristic of description rather than detail per se that makes it thick" (p. 255). More recently, Ponterotto (2006) has summarized thick description as referring to "the researcher's task of both describing and interpreting observed social action (or behavior) within its particular context." (p. 543).

Understanding and applying this evolving concept of thick description can be particularly challenging as it is much easier to grasp what it isn't than what it is. Providing pages of detailed facts does not make the description thick. Such chronological reporting of bulleted thin facts fails to capture the gestalt or whole of the observation and more likely weakens a description into disconnected fragmented parts, as you can see in the following:

The student walked into the library and sat down.

The student opened a book.

The student read the book.

The student departed the library.

Reporting such basic details is not only boring to read but provides limited information of value. Thick description, on the other hand, provides details which enrich our deeper understandings of events. The researcher constructs meanings from these observations to determine importance from within the information. The significance of an observation, event, or behavior is richer with the inclusion of voices, feelings, actions, and meanings (Ponterotto, 2006). By providing context, observed intent and alignment with the underlying purpose of the research study, a description can become much more than basic facts.

Denzin (1989) outlines important features of thick description which emerge when the researcher shares details:

- Biographical (Who?)
- Historical (What led to this?)
- Situational (What's the context?)
- Relational (What's happening?)
- Interactional (What are the meanings and relationships?)

What might a thick description look like? As you read the following example consider how you might approach the task of improving descriptive narrative in your own writing. This example was published by the National Academy of Sciences to assist health-care providers to better understand the use of thick description related to pain management (Donaldson & Mohr, 2001). These excerpts offer an abridged sample of thick description and thin description.

An Example of Thick Description—

"A lot of the nurses get stuck on getting a number—that may be hard for a patient. So, I get them to listen to what the patient says about the pain, not just a number. We can look at the pain rating, but also look at what the patient is doing and is able to do. The patient needs to understand that there are things that we can do, but sometimes we can't eliminate all pain. The pain scales have #1–10, but they also have word attached to the scale: 2 = mild, 5 = moderate, 8 = severe, 10 = worse possible. So, if a patient gives words, a number can be attached and it can be graphed.

We work on non-pharmacologic as well as pharmacologic interventions. A conversation with the patient assesses what level of pain is acceptable. A post-surgery patient, for example, should be able to breathe deeply and get up and walk and do more for themselves each day. A terminally-ill patient should be able to eat and visit with people. When a person has pain that is a 5 or more we have to talk with them to understand what that means. The nurse is learning and the patient is learning too so that they understand that this is not about how much pain can you stand. . . . You have to make it easy to do the right thing. It has to be easy to manage pain."

"After difficulty getting nurse and physician involvement, the site has focused on responsiveness to patients' pain. Site has pain algorithms, an interdisciplinary steering committee that sets goals, and wall charts to use in asking patients about their pain. Pain is charted as a vital sign and has become fairly well accepted, but pain management will need constant attention." (Used with permission of National Academies Press, from Appendix A, Example of Thin and Thick Description for Qualitative Analysis, of Exploring Innovation and Quality Improvement in Health Care Micro-Systems: A Cross-Case Analysis, M. S. Donaldson & J. J. Mohr, 2001; permission conveyed through Copyright Clearance Center, Inc.)

This chapter has offered strategies on how you might improve the quality of your data and how your use of data in your writing moves from description to interpretation. Hopefully, you have picked up some ideas on how you may adopt improvements in the management and presentation of high-quality credible findings from your data. The next chapter discusses the continued development of your writing from interpretation into the analysis process.

 # WRITING UP FINDINGS

This chapter is intended to get you thinking about how to use your writing to distill and express meaning in your research. The qualitative researcher draws findings from meanings which have been distilled from the data. Finding, building, and presenting meaningful connections in relationships you have identified in your data can really help the reader follow your story.

7.A DISTILLING EMERGENT MEANINGS

Now that you are working through your analysis, strive to look for subtle nuanced shifts and changes in intent among participants. As you move to distill emergent meaning in your work, use clear language and strive to promote disambiguation. When distilling meanings your aim is to present evidence transparently in a convincing and credible manner that goes beyond a replication of raw data (Jonsen et al., 2018; Pratt et al., 2019). To help achieve this, remember that language is incredibly important. Consider this:

As a novice researcher you enter a room and find many groups of researchers, all with different levels of experience talking freely in the language of your discipline. How do you react? If it were me, I would wander around the room listening from the outside of the groups and try to hear snippets of the conversations, gradually becoming more aware of the topics being spoken about. Once I have a clearer idea about which topics are being spoken about in which groups, the next step is to think about which group is talking about something close to my area of interest. Then hovering around this group, I would start to hear more details about what they are talking about, how they are talking about these topics, and some of the language specific to this discipline. Now I may hear something that connects specifically to my area of interest and I might ask a question or make a comment, and, perhaps when a little more familiar with the conversations in this group, I might join the conversation.

This is what you are doing when you write up your work—you are joining a conversation in your discipline. If you want your intended audience to read this work, you must use the appropriate language of the discipline. Remember words can be misinterpreted and have different meanings in different disciplines, so take care and choose your words well.

7.A.1 Dealing With Complex Meanings

The qualitative researcher must consider the social and cultural complexity of language. This requires awareness and sensitivity in reaching your intended audience by writing clearly and minimizing ambiguity. Of particular difficulty in presenting complex meanings is knowing when and how to use figurative expressions well, such as idioms, similes and metaphors like those in Table 7.1. Colloquial phrases and regional sayings often require clarification so that your intended meaning is delivered as you intended. Is your writing crystal clear or lost in translation? Did your writing make it out of the gate or is it dead as a doornail? Alas, such writing often muddies the water . . .

The following example can be used as a training exercise to consider how we interpret writing. It shows what appears to be an easily understood transcript, however the text can be understood in several different ways. This text is a challenging example of how researchers must be attuned to the context of the surrounding situation, as well as checking themselves for their own perceptions and worldview when they consider and draw meanings from data. Different understandings of the language can change based on your viewpoint, culture, background, research focus, socioeconomic status, audience, or jargon, among other factors. Beware of your assumptions and worldview as you write up your interpretations of data.

"It was a hot and sunny day, and everyone was feeling the heat. The classroom was airless, and it was making it difficult to concentrate. I had my hair tied back to try and keep its weight off my neck in this oppressive weather. I was always told that I was a **clever clogs**[1] but you wouldn't know it as I couldn't finish the test. The clock was moving slowly as we were all watching the big hand

TABLE 7.1 ■ Different Meanings in Language

Different Meanings in Language	
Idiom	Time to pull up stumps and end the meeting
Simile	She watched the room like a hawk
Metaphor	The classroom was a zoo
Colloquial phrase	Helicopter parent

waiting for it to reach the 12, which would mean lunch and time outside in the breezy cooler air. Then the teacher came around to collect the papers and looked at me and **smirked**[(2)]: "Can you go and **fetch my lunch?**"[(3)]. I felt a bit bothered by this and didn't know how to respond. I waited a few moments, then stood up and left the class."

Comments on text

[(1)] As a noun "**clever clogs**" can mean someone who is very clever, usually in a slightly annoying way; or "clogs" on its own can mean an obstruction, or a heavy, traditionally wooden-soled shoe. In the UK, "clever clogs" can also be used as a pejorative term (readers from another country may not know this).

[(2)] "She looked at me and **smirked**" can also have different meanings to different people. If considering a power relationship between a teacher and a student, it could mean that the teacher knew they were in control of the situation. In this example, the power dynamic between the teacher and the person sharing this story seems very imbalanced. It could also mean smiling in a way that expresses self-satisfied pleasure about a completed task, or knowing something that is not known by the other.

[(3)] "Can you go and **fetch my lunch**" seems to build on the ideas raised in the point above. What is going on here? As you read these words, did it make you feel uncomfortable? Do we know anything about the relationship between the teacher and this person, for example, are they related, how do they know each other?

To wrap up this discussion: is there any evidence in the example to say whether the person telling the story is male or female? Consider this carefully as nothing descriptive is mentioned, although in our experience most readers consider them to be female. Can you think how they come to this conclusion? Is this a cultural thing? Do you think they are female because they tied back their hair? Also consider whether the person telling the story is a student, a teacher's aide, or a classroom visitor. How did you come to this conclusion?

As you are writing, and as you keep writing, choose your words with care, as different words mean different things to different people.

7.A.2 Developing Connections During Analysis

This may be a point in your work when writing starts to become tricky. How do you find connections in your data? What are some strategies you can use to connect evidence and findings through writing? When you are stuck with your analysis, how can you move forward through writing?

The following Figure 7.1 shows how the process connects all the pieces. As you work with your data, you will be coding, grouping data, and categorizing and looking for patterns and meanings. All of these actions are connected, and it is your job as the writer to show how they are connected. As you identify connections and build relationships in the data your writing will continue to improve. You are now drawing upon a better understanding of the analytic process and can present clear steps which you are taking.

As you begin coding, you will spend a lot of time reviewing and developing your codes and their relationship to each other. Make sure that you write, and continue to write, many analysis memos so that you can keep track of your developing thinking. Capture any shifts from inductive thinking to deductive thinking in memos as well. Write as many memos as you can. However many memos you write, you can always write one more. As you capture this thought process it will be very helpful to you as you keep on writing. Remember a little bit each day and keep that momentum going . . .

> Remember: As many memos you write, it will never be enough. Memos are great to help you recreate your different lines of enquiry and remind you how you developed your findings as you write up your analysis process.

When you start to group your data, you will be comparing what you see, hear, and read, and redefining those groupings. This is an iterative process so don't think you must keep moving forward with this process—it is OK to go

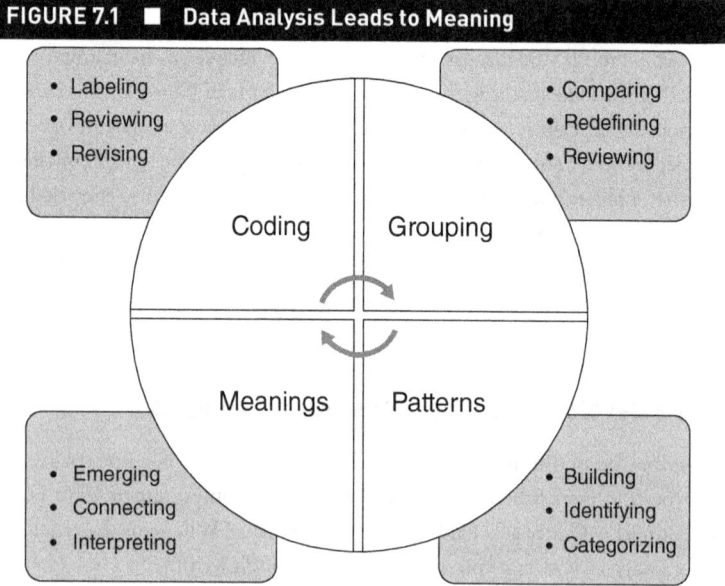

FIGURE 7.1 ■ Data Analysis Leads to Meaning

back and revisit coding as meaning starts to emerge. Coding is an evolving process with ongoing revisions as you merge, prune, and add new codes. Each code definition must also be updated and revised as your work progresses. As you keep working through this process, writing as you go, patterns will become clearer. Here you are really starting to build your message and develop a clearer understanding of what you want to say. Keep writing about this as you move through the process and have faith that meanings will emerge through writing. Writing is the way you keep track of how your thinking is developing and it always helps to have a written record to revisit in the future.

Remember to keep writing as you start to map connections; in this way meanings start to emerge. Whether each piece of writing ends up in the final product doesn't matter—all writing has value as you tell your story.

7.A.3 Showing Relationships in Your Data

When writing up the findings of any study, it is good to do so with tables and figures showing connections and relationships in the data. For example, Table 7.2 is an example showing how different findings in the study are linked to the data sources in the same study. This can really help the reader visually follow along with your analysis leading to your findings. Now challenge yourself to think of other ways you can visually show what is happening in your data and your analysis. Develop charts and tables as you go, and keep records of all iterations of all diagrams. You will be surprised what ends up in your final story.

To be able to do this successfully, it is important to start capturing this thinking early in the process. It is extremely hard to create a table such as Table 7.2 when you are almost finished; it much easier to do this as you go. This is only one

TABLE 7.2 ■ Linking Data Sources to Findings

Data Source	Finding #1	Finding #2	Finding #3	Finding #4
Interviews	X		X	X
Focus groups		X		
Observations	X	X	X	
Documents		X	X	X
Methods memos	X	X		
Analytic memos	X	X	X	X
Reflection memos	X		X	

Source: Kaczynski, Salmona, & Smith (2014). Reproduced with permission.

example of a visual that you might use to show the connections in your data; you must find the visuals that work well for you. One way to do this is to doodle as you go through the process and create simple diagrams that capture the way you are thinking. Keep a record of all these diagrams and you may find as you move through iterations of draft writing that you revisit earlier diagrams and continue to update them. These are likely to end up in your final piece of writing.

7.B DATA ANALYSIS AND INTERPRETATION THROUGH WRITING

This section considers how to distill and cook down your data to its essence, and then interpret that in your own voice as a researcher through writing. Data distillation is a process of deriving meaning from raw data; taking the complex raw data and distilling the complex knowledge into more accessible findings—building a framework for communicating the essence of what you are interpreting from your data. This sounds tricky and it is. However, if you write as you go, you can often begin to see patterns developing.

A surprising large amount of analysis occurs as you are writing. Data analysis memos can help, and they also become data as you keep on going through the analysis process. Writing up ideas as they come to you is important, so you keep track of your developing thinking and keep a trail for later review.

TABLE 7.3 ■ Qualitative Data Analysis Process

Qualitative Data Analysis Process	
Defining and identifying	Identify and gather the data required to answer the research question/s and focus of the study.
Gathering and storing	Store and categorize the raw data for ease of analysis.
Reduction and sampling	Filter the data for relevance to the research question/s.
Coding	Categorize the data by assigning labels through coding. Write a definition for each code. Coding is a first step in the analysis and acts as a foundation for higher levels of analysis and meaning generation.
Grouping	Through coding you will begin to distill and group your data and redefining those groups through an iterative process, Revisit the coding as you go through this process.

TABLE 7.3 ■ Qualitative Data Analysis Process *(Continued)*

Qualitative Data Analysis Process

Finding patterns and constructing meaning	Insight into the research question/s are obtained through saturation. At this point you are reasonably assured that further data collection would yield similar results and serve to confirm emerging themes. It is the point in a qualitative research project when there is enough data to ensure the research questions can be answered. Meaning can emerge through writing.
Writing up findings	Construct your argument based on your findings, drawing on what you have done, what you have seen and what you have heard. These conclusions will contribute to the body of knowledge and represent new meaning and insight into the research questions.

Qualitative research is by its very nature messy. It is the researcher's job to find structure and meaning so that they can tell the story of the research to the reader (Table 7.3). A structured writing process will aid you in avoiding the writing trap of getting bogged down in too much detail about how you are analyzing the data and more about sharing what you discovered and found from your analysis.

> Often-asked questions by novice writers are "How do you add participant quotations into your work?" and "How many extracts from the participant voice do you need in your analysis?" These are very tricky questions to answer, however, the following points may help.
>
> - Fewer quotes, more interpretation
>   - Focus on fewer quotes as evidence
>   - Show the audience how this quote is important in your work
>   - Highlight key words if it helps to tell the story of your research
>   - Provide interpretation about each quote to locate it in your work
>
> - If the quote is important enough for you to include in your work, make sure you explain this importance clearly to the reader
>
> - Any included quote is evidence and becomes part of your story

The following are suggested readings for further information into the qualitative data analysis process:

Bazeley, P. (2020). *Qualitative data analysis: Practical strategies* (2nd ed.). SAGE.
Cannella, G. S., Pérez, M. S., & Pasque, P. A. (Eds.). (2016). *Critical qualitative inquiry: Foundations and futures*. Routledge.

Denzin, N. K., & Lincoln, Y. S. (Eds.). (2018). *The SAGE handbook of qualitative research* (5th ed.). SAGE.

Gibson, W., & Brown, A. (2009). *Working with qualitative data.* SAGE.

LeCompte, M. D. (2000). Analyzing qualitative data. *Theory into Practice, 39*(3), 146–154.

Maxwell, J. A. (2013). *Qualitative research design: An interactive approach* (3rd ed.). SAGE.

Richards, L. (2021). *Handling qualitative data: A practical guide* (4th ed.). SAGE.

Schram, T. H. (2006). *Conceptualizing and proposing qualitative research* (2nd ed.). Merrill Prentice Hall.

Having discussed writing up findings in this chapter, this next section presents the reflections of an early career academic on writing up findings in her dissertation. As you read this next section, think about your own work, and take some time to reflect on what you can learn from reading about Sara's journey as a developing qualitative researcher.

7.C A RESEARCHER'S REFLECTIONS ON WRITING UP FINDINGS

REFLECTIONS ON MY FINDINGS SECTION: PRESENTING PARTICIPANT QUOTES

BY SARA E. GRUMMERT

Institute for Mixed Methods Research

Introduction

Writing up research findings is a creative, nonlinear process that is one of the most fun, and challenging, stages of the research process. Below I reflect on how I presented my research findings based on my experience writing my dissertation, a qualitative study of college athlete experiences with various mechanisms of discipline, surveillance, and punishment within their athletic departments (Grummert, 2021).

After I completed coding my qualitative interview data, I was faced with seemingly innumerable ways to present the data to my audience. Though my reflection is merely one example, the strategies behind how to present themes and participant quotes may help inform your own thinking about how to best communicate your findings to the reader.

Organizing Themes

After I completed coding of 20 interviews, I had over 900 coded excerpts that I needed to distill into digestible themes. Memoing throughout the analysis process helped scaffold my thinking about larger themes and which thematic categories codes fell under. For example, Chapter 5, "Surveillance, Discipline, and Punishment," included coded data that represented three large themes: Surveillance, Discipline, Punishment. Each theme encapsulated more specific codes such as class checks, progress reports, social media restrictions, drug testing, and boosters (see Figure 7.2 below). I used Dedoose (2022), a qualitative and mixed methods data analysis application, to code these interviews. Doing so made it easy to view, visualize connections and export participant quotes along each thematic category in order to assess which participant quotes would be useful to present to the reader, as well as which participant experiences I could summarize for the reader.

FIGURE 7.2 ■ Themes and codes for participant interviews

Surveillance	Punishment
Class Checks, Progress Reports, Drug Testing, Social Media, Boosters	Emotional, Physical, Material, Denial of Autonomy

Organizing Themes

It was important to find a balance between my own writing voice and presenting and honoring my participants' voices throughout the writing process. I knew it was important for me as the researcher to do the translational and interpretative work of applying and connecting theory to participant quotes as I presented them, and it was equally important each participant story was represented and their experiences maintained the core focus of the research. I used various strategies for presenting participant quotes according to the theme and the theoretical significance that I was communicating to my audience. For example, when I asked participants about their experiences with health professionals and if they trusted team doctors, I included the range of responses from several participants to highlight the stark contrast between Black and nonblack participants:

> When I asked each participant if they trusted team doctors, the responses from Black participants were in stark contrast to nonblack participants. Black participants overwhelming responded with a negative such as "no," "hell no," "not at all," "no, clearly no," and "I can't trust nobody," whereas nonblack participants overwhelmingly answered with an affirmative "yes," "absolutely," "definitely," "yeah, for sure," and "wholeheartedly." Some nonblack participants even expanded, unprompted, about how

much they felt cared for and in trusted hands with medical staff. (Grummert, 2021, p. 116)

In that short excerpt, I presented responses from 12 out of 20 participants. The strategy of presenting short quotes across several participants highlighted the magnitude of their different experiences falling into one of two categories (i.e., those who were treated well by team doctors and those who were not) and allowed me more space to write about the significance of their responses overall. In this case, my voice was much more present in the writing as I was condensing and summarizing many responses, rather than relying on one or two participant quotes to relay the finding to the reader.

Conversely, I used the strategy of presenting one participant's experience in-depth to communicate an important finding about accessing quality healthcare (Grummert, 2021, pp. 105–108). Presenting lengthy or longer quotes from one participant was useful for cases in which (a) one participant shared a vivid, detailed story that spoke to my research questions and/or highlighted specific aspects of an experience that was also referenced by other participants; (b) I simply could not state the point better than the participant did themselves; and/or (c) the participant had an experience that was an outlier compared to other participants that was important to include for transparency and/or complemented other research findings.

In the case of Ari, I spent several pages sharing Ari's experience of attempting to get healthcare for a medical problem that was being dismissed and ignored by her coach and team doctors. Since Black women throughout my study referenced the departmental negligence they faced when it came to their health, Ari sharing a detailed account of the nuances and barriers she faced to getting quality care was simply something I could not have summarized for the reader on her behalf. Presenting her story in its full form allowed the reader to get a better sense of the harm she faced and how she was personally affected from those experiences over time (the emotional toll and magnitude of which would have been difficult for me to translate to the reader myself).

Revising

As I revised my findings sections, there were several questions I asked myself such as:
- Which participants are represented in each section?
- Does this quote speak to my research questions or theoretical framework?
- Am I communicating enough context around participant quotes?
- When using one quote, is it representative of other participant experiences or an outlier?
- Am I presenting a mix of quotes across participants, or highlighting one or a few cases?
- Am I explaining the significance of quotes as I present them?

> These questions helped me reflect deeper on *how* I was representing my data to the reader as well as *why* I was choosing some strategies over others. Doing so helped me revise my findings in a more systematic manner, deepened my analysis, and helped me find my own writing voice throughout the findings. More importantly, engaging in this iterative process for each of my chapters about findings, allowed me to assess if I was successfully assembling and translating the coded data into a coherent narrative that answered my research questions and had explanatory power. (Grummert, 2023. Reproduced with permission.)

The reflective vignette by Sara Grummert (2023) has hopefully provided insights into several important concepts which have been highlighted in this book. Applying Dedoose as a digital tool was demonstrated and the challenges of identifying and expressing a writing voice were explored. The overall importance of building and presenting trustworthy credible findings was ultimately a driving reflective force in this work. You are now encouraged to take time to think about your research design and your data as you move toward writing up your conclusions and recommendations. Chapter 8 discusses delivering value through your research and how to build credibility for your research.

8 WRITING UP CONCLUSIONS AND RECOMMENDATIONS

This chapter explores strategies to strengthen the quality and credibility of your writing. There are several important issues that need to be addressed as you write up your findings and make connections back to your research questions, research purpose and focus. Consider, for example, how do your findings stand with and apart from the literature? Return to your study's foundational literature and consider how this groundwork informs your findings and recommendations. This step is an essential component of the research writing process which this chapter now discusses. Getting the most from using a literature map and concept map diagrams is also further considered. Once the results of the study are complete, you can create a final concept map that can become the basis for presenting a useful visual model in your subsequent discussion. By using diagrams to review your earlier writing you can refine the story of the study and clarify how the path of inquiry has evolved. Remember to retain each version of diagrams to corroborate your trail of the study path.

8.A DELIVERING VALUE

At this stage of your writing, you have invested considerable scholarly capital into crafting a credible study with meaning and are now pondering if, and how, your writing can best connect to others. Good qualitative writers strive to be seen and cited by an engaged audience. Goals such as these, help you push your writing to a higher level. To make such advancements in your writing you must demonstrate value to others. Value requires the delivery of worth or usefulness to those others you have set out to reach. *Value* is a powerful term which has unfortunately become overused by commercialized sales marketing and media. That said, there remains a fundamental aspect to value which must be retained in quality writing. Value is about connecting the perceived wants of an audience and finding ways to meet others where they are. One way to view this is to see yourself as both a qualitative writer and an educator. You retain the role and duties of an educator through your writing as you attempt to inform others. Value comes from the consumption of your writing. If the reader does not understand or connect with your message, then you have failed to teach as a writer educator.

> Question: Have you successfully fulfilled your intended goals and sufficiently addressed?
> - Answering the so what factor
> - Making meaningful connections
> - Demonstrating that your work has importance
> - Offering support for a greater social good

You may be asking yourself, at this point, how to measure the worth or usefulness of your writing. Carefully consider what steps you have taken to position your study and your writing to benefit others and less about how this work may benefit you. Knowing the value as measured by others underlies such judgements. This is not about the metrics of counting citations or publications, rather, producing qualitative work intended to confront a social problem and providing strategies which strive to promote a greater good. Essentially, you are asking yourself what have you offered that helps others? Make every effort to define success and value based on others, not yourself. An important step in doing this is to ensure that you have clearly articulated and described your well-defined audience in your writing. It is your responsibility to help your readers recognize the alignment you are building between who you (implicitly) think they are and what strategies you are recommending for their consideration and adoption.

8.B QUALITATIVE CONCLUSIONS

How do you transition your findings, which you formed during data analysis, to writing up your final recommendations and conclusions? Where does your discussion fit into this writing? Have you kept your story arc credible and convincing as you move from findings to the potential implications of your work? There are several important issues to consider as you write the concluding sections of your research.

8.B.1 Discussing Your Work

Writers may confuse where different types of discussions fit into their work. It is your job to draw distinctions between discussion about your findings and discussion of any recommendations drawn from the study. In the first case, discussion is the reporting out of analysis, and in the second case you are aligning your discussion with conclusions. In the latter case, you are not restating your findings and analysis, you are drawing from the implications of your findings and supporting literature to strengthen your story about your research, providing a stronger case for the arguments you are making.

> Moving from: Findings → Conclusions → Value to intended audience

At this point in your work, capturing what you have done in your study through diagrams or tables may help. Consider showing how you connected your data to the research questions; and how you can link your data sources to your findings (discussed earlier in Section 7.A.3, Showing Relationships in Your Data). The following table adapted from Kaczynski et al. (2014) can help you find a way to move from findings to conclusions. This is the goal in this chapter: moving your writing from findings to valuable conclusions. Table 8.1 may give you some ideas about how to present your research journey in a credible way, so that the audience can see how you moved from research

TABLE 8.1 ■ Connecting the Data and the Research Questions

Data Types	Data Sources	Connecting Data to Research Questions
Interviews	P1, P2, FG1	Show how the interview questions align to the research questions/s, e.g., Interview Qus 1–5 are related to Research Qu 3
Observations	Stock exchange Planning Meetings	These observations are related to Research Qu 4 These observations are related to Research Qu 6
Documents	Legislation Annual Reports	Show how this legislation helps answer research question/s, e.g., Evidence supporting the study focus
Memos	M1-8 A1-12 R1-6	Audit trail of emergent design Findings and interpretation of multiple meanings Research as instrument reflections

P = participant, FG = focus groups, M = methods, A = analytic, R = reflections

Source: Adapted from Kaczynski, Salmona, & Smith (2014). Reproduced with permission.

design through analysis to findings and conclusions. Building a table such as this will strengthen the transparency and credibility of your work.

You interpret the results for your audience in the Discussion section. Begin by taking the reader back to the research questions and discuss whether your findings answered these questions. You can use tables to help your reader make these connections. Make sure to highlight any unexpected or exciting results and link them to the research question. Also note that absence of an idea can be as important as presence, so consider earlier studies and draw comparisons on how your study is similar or different.

> Your goal is to show your study is trustworthy by establishing that your findings are credible, transferable, confirmable, and dependable (Lincoln & Guba, 1985; Patton, 2015, p. 685).
>
> - *Credibility* is a level of confidence in the study's findings: "How do you know that your findings are strong?" "How can you show that your findings reflect the views of the participants?" (Triangulation can help here.)
> - *Transferability* is how you show that your findings are applicable to other settings with similar participants, for example, similar situations, similar phenomena, and similar populations. (Thick description can help here.)
> - *Confirmability* is the extent that the authors' conclusions are logical, showing that the study's findings are based on participants' responses and not any potential researcher bias. (An audit trail showing that the findings represent participants' responses can help here)
> - *Dependability* is the degree that the study can be repeated by others with consistent findings. (Documenting the steps you took, and the decisions you made during analysis, can help here)

Before moving into conclusions, review your work and consider the following questions: Have I written clearly about complex topics? Have I tied disparate ideas together? These are difficult skills to master, and you can improve by writing, rewriting and rewriting again.

8.B.2 Composing Conclusions or Recommendations

In qualitative writing, the term *conclusion* is often applied in different ways and expressed using variations sharing similar meanings. Qualitative research is more about inquiry, discovery, and exploration which you undertake as a means to find deeper insights rather than a particular truth. As expressed in popular culture, *it is the journey, not the destination.* Knowing when and where to conclude a qualitative study is often more an issue of simply running out of time and energy. You don't conclude a qualitative study; at best, you find a good place to wrap it up. Qualitative researchers may experience troubling challenges if they strive to conclude their writing by building toward a dramatic climax with a grand flourish (Wolcott, 2001b, p. 120). Wolcott cautions that qualitative writers are "particularly vulnerable to the tendency and urge to go beyond reporting *what is* and to use their studies as platforms for making pronouncements of *what ought to be* (p. 121)." Rather than building toward a tight climax which likely creates a false sense of closure, his advice is that the qualitative writer give more attention to the presentation of what they found as perplexing as they pondered the essential issues of the study.

Consider the following two types of usage of the term *conclusion*. The first type of conclusion is applied as the last step in the data analysis process where the researcher is discussing and drawing meanings from findings. The second type of conclusion can be applied to the closing remarks which frame the final recommendations section of a research study. In this second type, you are drawing together the main points of your argument to concisely present the importance of your work. In this second type of meaning, you are striving to present a "sense of closure" for your audience (Evans & Gruba, 2002, p. 121). In addition, this second type of usage commonly encompasses recommendations for further study and suggested changes in practice. In this chapter, the first type of usage is referred to as **drawing conclusions** and the second type as **conclusions and recommendations**.

Once you have presented and fully discussed your findings from your study and connected this discussion back to the literature, it is now time to *draw conclusions*. This is the beginning of the end to your story. Remember, every point raised in the conclusion must connect to your story arc and it is OK if that story arc is refined and modified. These refinements are an important step to ensure cohesive alignment. Although time consuming, it is important to now go back and weave and polish the final story arc from start to end.

Each conclusion drawn from your analysis of data represents a finding that is based on evidence which you have gathered. As you craft conclusions from a given finding, you may find that readers can draw more than a single point of importance if you provide the broader implications of your finding. This is particularly relevant in qualitative writing as the analysis process promotes the exploration of multiple meanings. Qualitative research is fraught with ambiguity which often leaves both you and your audience perplexed. As Wolcott (2001b) suggests, rather than striving for a tight satisfying closure, you may find it more constructive to explain that the meanings from your work are not all that clear (p. 122). From here, your writing can then discuss recommendations and implications. Also note that a conclusion drawn from the findings will be built upon the literature which you have previously woven into your discussion about your findings. Your discussion of meanings extends your findings beyond what has been previously recognized by others and builds the main argument of your study forward, ideally offering new insights.

Composing the conclusions and recommendations section of your work requires attention to important distinctions. Crisp concise brevity must be your goal as you compose your final thoughts (Evans & Gruba, 2002). Here the conclusion will avoid raising new points or making new claims which lack an empirical foundation which you did not provide earlier. If you find yourself wanting to cover new ground, consider framing a new point as a potential path for future work. Clearly frame this new point as an important issue worthy of further consideration that reaches beyond the scope of this particular study.

It is worth carefully considering what different audiences might be seeking from your conclusions and recommendations which you are drawing from your study. Strive to deliver the main points of your work in an audience specific manner to optimize the impact and diffusion of your research findings (Higginbottom, 2015). To achieve this, you will need to stay open to the perspectives and viewpoints of others. Your readers will likely interpret your work based on how they apply your insights to their own research and writings. Give consideration and ponder the importance of these broader implications as you further refine meanings and draw conclusions.

8.B.3 Referencing the Literature

Referencing the literature in the conclusions and recommendations section is likely, yet again, another challenging step in writing for you to confront. This step is often misunderstood by doctoral candidates and early career researchers. It is also occasionally overlooked by experienced researchers as well. At this point in your writing, you have something interesting to say about your research as you begin building upon the findings from your analysis. It is very important at this stage to circle back and discuss your findings against the literature (Dunne, 2011; Dunne & Buse, 2020; Machi & McEvoy, 2016). Avoid repeating what you have already written about the literature that informs your study, rather write about both common ground and divergence. Based on your literature review, did you find what you expected to find? Was something missing that you expected?

> Remember absence can be just as important as presence when discussing your qualitative findings while referencing the foundational literature for your study.

Chapter 8 • Writing up Conclusions and Recommendations   103

As you immerse yourself in reading the literature, your ideas can get lost or suppressed by the polished and refined writing of others which you have identified during your search of published work. You may feel like the writings by published authors express important issues much better than you can. This feeling likely connects to a notion that you cannot write as well as these other authors which you have found in the literature. To confront this feeling, you need to find and use your voice and remember that your study is unique. Continue to remind yourself that your work stands apart from this supporting foundation material and your intent is to shed new light into a particular aspect into the topic.

A related challenge you may confront as you weave literature into your writing is when the presentation of literature is reduced to a superficial reporting process. This is similar to simply providing an expanded annotated bibliography. Applying the literature to your work is much more than providing a detailed summary of the work of others. If you find that you are inserting long quotes from the literature, then you may likely be struggling with bringing your voice into the discussion. This is particularly troublesome when you insert a long quote and neglect to follow with your own writing explaining how this reference is particular germane to your line of argument. It is your missing voice that is needed to extend the argument about the important issues which you are bringing to light. Remember that you are creating knowledge through your writing rather than merely serving as a knowledge recorder (Ondrusek, 2012). Your research is extending the readers understandings of new knowledge beyond a collection of previously published texts.

8.C BUILDING CREDIBILITY USING QUALITY INDICATORS

Building a credible and convincing story arc requires weaving a complete picture from start to finish. This demands investing a bit more time into ensuring a consistent presentation of high-quality findings and conclusions. Take the time now to further refine and edit your presentation of unique insights into a social problem that you have invested considerable work into researching. By taking these steps, your writing has the potential to inform real-life policies, social programs, and professional practices.

One way to approach this review is to return to the beginning and ask yourself if your study consistently presents well-conceived and clearly articulated research questions that reflects a genuine appreciation of some mystery that is best answered using qualitative research methodology (Lieber, 2016, p. 2). Articulating the value of your chosen methods must support the research focus and ultimately the conclusions of this work. Here you are articulating the value of your chosen research design by critically showing that your unique approach is the best way to answer the questions and provide credible recommendations.

The following points may help you identify weak areas that require further attention. Your goal during this review process is to seek the highest quality writing. When reviewing your work from start to finish ask yourself:

- Is the focus statement consistent throughout?
- Are the research questions clearly articulated?
- Does the study demonstrate open-minded but disciplined inquiry?
- Is the research method and design well chosen?
- How do the findings support the conclusions?
- Is there confidence in the findings and conclusions?
- Is the argument clear and consistent (refer to section 5B)?

Table 8.2 (which was introduced in Chapter 1) is drawn from the work of Ondrusek (2012, p. 179) who reviewed the literature and identified 12 core competencies which are considered essential for advanced writing skills.

This list presents key competencies in three main groups: mechanics and grammar (1–5), design thinking (6–7), and credibility and quality (8–12). You might find it helpful to think about your writing using these three groups when reviewing your work. Start with mechanics and grammar as you move through to quality. Break down each piece of your writing and review; consider where your strengths and weaknesses lie; and find out where you can get help to improve any deficiencies in your writing. It is interesting when reviewing this listing of writing abilities that although mechanics and grammar are important, the top three essential skills involve building a convincing argument with a clear voice. As Johnson et al., (2020) say, the "key to quality reporting of qualitative research results are clarity, organization, completeness, accuracy, and conciseness in communicating the results to the reader" (p. 144).

As a writer, consider strengthening the credibility in your writing by sharing your storyline with others for constructive feedback. Through such

TABLE 8.2 ■ **Core Competencies for Advanced Writing Skills**

Core Competencies for Advanced Writing Skills	
1	organization
2	argument/evidence/logic
3	audience/voice
4	content
5	mechanics/grammar
6	conceptualization/developing ideas/prewriting
7	process
8	accuracy
9	scholarly identity
10	sources
11	expression
12	critique

Source: Adapted from Ondrusek (2012, p. 179).

collaboration you will identify areas requiring improvements which will both enhance clarity and strengthen your arguments.

Critically assess the relevance of your writing by considering quality indicators for your work. When working with journals, consider the following quality indicators: the number of times the article is cited, which will indicate the level of discipline interest triggered by the article; the journal's impact factor to compare the journal to others in the field; and the author's h-index which is based on the researcher's most cited papers and the number of citations that they have received in other publications. Also consider the journal's credibility by investigating where the journal is indexed:

- Is the journal indexed in the major databases for the field?
- How long has the journal been around?
- Who is on the editorial board?
- How diligent is the peer-review process?

This chapter began with a discussion about writing conclusions and moved directly into a conversation on quality and credibility. Underlying the drawing and presentation of meaningful conclusions requires a delivery of value and effectively demonstrating the steps you have taken to ensure your work is of high quality. Remember that you must carefully consider what steps you have taken to position your study and your writing to benefit others and less about how this work may benefit you. The next chapter explores a remaining challenge of sharing your work with others.

9 SHARING THE STORY OF YOUR RESEARCH WITH OTHERS

As you move through your final revision and think ahead to sharing the story of your research with your audience, consider that readers must be able to find, select, and index your work. An engaging title and strong abstract, either descriptive or informative, allows readers who may be interested in a longer work to quickly decide whether it is worth their time to read your piece among many others they may find. Good titles and abstracts emphasize the central topics of the work and gives prospective readers enough information to make an informed judgment about the applicability of the work. Also, many online databases use abstracts to index larger works, so you must be sure that your title and abstract contain keywords and phrases that allow for easy searching and appropriate discovery.

9.A REVISION STRATEGIES

At this stage of your writing, hopefully you will notice your work improving after each revision. Yet writers often struggle as they near the end to set aside sufficient time to bring themselves to read their work carefully from start to finish. An effective strategy to overcome this hesitancy is to begin by giving yourself a break. Walk away from your completed draft for a few days or preferably a week if you can. With fresh eyes and a clear mind, come back and begin a critical review, in a similar manner as that of an editor. As taxing as this may be, start at the beginning and read to the end, line by line. When attempting a complete reading, remember to flag all mark-ups as you go (with track changes, or comments) so that you can return and spend time cleaning up and clarifying troubling sections.

When reading as an editor, give particular attention to identifying loose ends and incomplete thoughts. You may find it helpful to mentally assume a frame of mind of that of your intended audience. As you undertake this critical review, you are performing more than a reading for grammatical correctness. You are looking for gaps and possible misunderstanding around complex issues and concepts which may be misconstrued. Challenge yourself by considering if you have expressed important points exactly as you intended. As you unpack and unravel these knotted sections the narrative flow will improve and you will find that you are more effectively reaching your audience. If you find a sentence that is five lines long, or the length of a paragraph, it is good idea to find a way to simplify this complexity and single out each of the different points into a sentence of their own.

> An editing technique that you may find helpful is to scan for sections where *The* is repeatedly used to start sentences. This may be an indicator that you have not fully developed a clear train of thought. Note that this mistake may be accompanied by one sentence paragraphs. The following demonstrates how overuse of *The* obscures and weakens writing quality.
>
> **The** *different teaching strategies highlighted how curriculum development needed to be adapted to* **the** *classroom setting to ensure that* **the** *instructional practices were effective rather than just being novel.* **The** *teachers connected their existing pedagogical tools to* **the** *new methods and demonstrated useful ways for them to build confidence and expertise as they continued through* **the** *process.* **The** *level of engagement that* **the** *teachers described also demonstrated* **the** *changes in practice.*

Another issue of concern is uncovering possible stray arguments. Here you are looking for breaks and unintended paths of diversion from the story arc. This can be analogous to going down unintended rabbit holes. Although you may find a particular point interesting to ponder, once you follow the path you discover that you are lost in a maze with no way back to the story arc. Your writing will improve if you cut your losses and walk away from that diversionary train of thought. By the way, this reminds me of the time I found a rabbit hole in the forest . . .

A final revision strategy for your consideration is the importance of removing written material that is no longer relevant to the study. This is particularly difficult for the writer as you have already invested considerable time and energy into this material. You need to make this tough call and cut it out if it no longer relates to the intended message of your work.

9.B MAKING YOUR WORK EASY TO FIND AND GETTING READY FOR PUBLICATION

Your writing is almost finished with your final story arc carefully woven throughout. It is time to revisit your title to make sure it reflects where your writing has ended. It is also time to write the abstract for your study. These are both key tasks which are completed at the close, not the beginning. By writing the title and abstract at the end, you will more accurately present your finished work for publication and make it easy to find by others.

9.B.1 Title: How to Identify and Use Keywords

When you started your writing, you began with a working title. Now consider how your work has evolved and what key words may be most appropriate. Key words are best when easily searchable.

Good keywords can be used by search engines to help find relevant papers. If you choose strong keywords, database search engines will be able to find your work, and, readers will be able to find it too. On the plus side, this will probably increase the number of people reading your manuscript, and likely lead to more citations. These key terms can act like a brief one to two-word summary of your work and they make your writing searchable so that others can cite your work. As you develop your key words you might think about it from the point of view of the reader and consider what terms they might use as a search term when conducting a literature review.

> Choose your keywords carefully so that they
> - Characterize the content of your manuscript
> - Are discipline specific to your field of research

When you have your key words, use them to develop a title, and then road test this title with others.

A good title does several things:

- First, it predicts content.
- Second, it catches the reader's interest.
- Third, it reflects the tone or slant of the piece of writing.
- Fourth, it contains keywords that will make it easy to access by a computer search. (Hairston & Keen, 2003, p. 73)

Keeping these functions in mind will help you choose a specific and meaningful title, rather than a mere label for your work.

A good title is one of the most important elements of your writing as it begins to inform and convince your readers. A clear title shows that your writing does what you say it does and will capture the readers' interest and attention. It gives your audience an indication of the main idea of your writing and allows you to articulate your argument. Having a working title throughout the process can help you stay on track; revisiting the title at the end of the process can help you make sure the central argument of your writing is clear. It is likely that you will write and rewrite your title several times to make it as informative as possible. Finding the perfect, eye-catching title is not always possible. Just do the best you can to find a title that conveys your message to your audience and invites them to read your work (see Table 9.1 for some ideas to get you started).

Most titles have the same basic structure. It is your job to craft a hook: the creative element that catches the eye of the reader and encourages them to read your work. A successful title may be a phrase that is catchy such as a play on words that draws the reader to your writing. As titles are often in two parts, the hook can be in either the basic title or the subtitle. You might even develop this hook from your key terms.

Here are two examples of titles which have extensive citations, likely (in part) due to their eye-catching keyword phrases:

TABLE 9.1 ■ Qualities to Look for in a Good Title

Qualities of a Good Title	
Effective	The title will describe the main topic in your writing and highlight the importance of your work. It will be concise and attract readers to your work.
Believable	Make your title catchy so that it captures the interest of your audience. However, don't stray from the truth. Make sure that your title outlines what the audience will find when they read your work.
Eye-catching	An eye-catching title is better than a boring title but not always possible. Do the best you can. One way to do this is to use an active voice, rather than a passive one.
Accurate	Always make sure that your title is accurate and gives a clear idea about what your audience will be reading in your work.
Brief	Brief titles are easy to follow and concise. Long titles can be confusing. You may find yourself somewhere in between and that's OK too. Keep the title straightforward and uncomplicated, use accessible language and stay away from complicated phrases.

Salmona, M., & Kaczynski, D. (2016). **Don't blame the software: Using qualitative data analysis software successfully in doctoral research**. Forum Qualitative Sozialforschung/*Forum: Qualitative Social Research*, 17(3), Art. 11, http://nbn-resolving.de/urn:nbn:de:0114-fqs1603117

Lieber, E., Chin, D, Nihira, K., & Mink, I. T. (2001). **Holding on and letting go: Identity and acculturation among Chinese immigrants**. *Cultural Diversity and Ethnic Minority Psychology*, 7(3), 247–261. doi:10.1037/1099-9809.7.3.247 PMID: 11506071.

9.B.2 Writing a Strong Abstract

It may seem odd that the last section of your writing is the first section read by your audience. Writing the abstract is best done after you have completed your work. An abstract quickly summarizes the main points of the paper that follows; it needs to be a succinct summary of your work. Abstracts for professional journals are typically anywhere from 150 to 300 words depending on where you are submitting your work. The maximum word count does not include citations. Given these restrictive word counts, making the most of the small space you have for your abstract will determine how successful you are at highlighting the important facets of your writing. As Conte (n.d.) emphasizes, "the abstract is perhaps the most important section of your manuscript." Although it is a brief summary, the abstract represents the gateway to your entire effort.

The function of the abstract is to convince the reader that your work is worth the investment of their time. Typically abstracts are the part of the article freely available. When researching work, researchers may only read your abstract, so it must stand alone and provide an accurate summary of your work. If you write a strong and clear abstract, it will encourage researchers to read your full paper. Your goal is to help researchers who are reviewing full abstracts from online searching services find what they need.

A strong abstract will

- Clearly and concisely summarize your writing,
- Be a time-saving shortcut for busy researchers, and
- Point your readers to the most important parts of your written content.

A good abstract will answer these questions:

- What was done?
- Why did you do it?

- What did you find?

- How are these findings useful and important?

Different audiences will require different formats for the abstract. For example, a professional journal will give specific instructions for a research article; and a university will give required instructions for an abstract for a dissertation. Conference abstracts are different again as they will require to build on the conference theme. The abstract for the dissertation is likely to be longer than a journal article, as it is for a much longer work.

Most publisher websites provide publication requirements with an author link announcing a call for papers or submission gateway. These links typically include important requirements and resources for authors to use when writing an abstract. An example of a comprehensive resource guide tutorial on writing an abstract is provided on the Springer publications website (SpringerLink Publishers, n.d.). In addition to discussing abstracts the Springer tutorial includes guidance with titles and keywords.

As well as the writing centers at universities, most universities also provide specific resources to help you develop your abstract. Some examples include Penn State University, Graduate Writing Center; Purdue University, OWL writing report abstracts; Carnegie Mellon University, how to write an abstract; and The University of North Carolina at Chapel Hill writing center abstracts. Search online for university abstract resources and see what is available.

9.C REACHING A LARGER AUDIENCE

"Research is of no use unless it gets to the people who need to use it" (Whitty, 2019). You need to recognize that reaching the appropriate audience is your responsibility. Researchers often communicate and share their research with other academic scholars through peer-reviewed journal articles and presentations. There may, however, be others that would benefit from you sharing your findings through news releases, social media, social and government policy releases, community organization websites, and other key groups. Sharing your work can help others improve professional practices and inform social policy decision making. Think about the intended purpose behind your writing and what you originally set out to share. Are you trying to raise awareness of a particular issue? Are you inviting engagement and feedback? Who do you want your research to reach and for what purpose? Who will find your research most valuable?

Think about, and create a dissemination plan for your work: a step-by-step process that starts by identifying what your message could look like, and with whom you might share your work. This plan will give you a structure to help you guide the timing and delivery style for each message.

1. Identify and describe your objectives and goals for sharing your work.

2. Determine your target audience: Study participants, media outlets, community groups, policymakers. Remember to use an existing channel for a group if possible (see #3).

3. Identify communication channels you might use for your different audiences. Remember to tailor your message and materials to each audience—keep this message short and succinct, use non-technical language, and highlight the key points to help your audience clearly understand your findings.

4. Provide conclusions and suggestions about making your findings relevant to professional practitioners or social policy decision makers.

Don't limit yourself to thinking about using the written or spoken word. Introduce visual elements, such as graphic representations, into your work that help your audience interpret and understand your writing. Lastly, you need to find the right tools to help you share your work, for example, tools to help create innovative visuals (e.g., DataHero, Plot.ly), crowdsourcing and collaboration platforms (e.g., Thinklab), networking platforms (e.g., ORCID), and publishing platforms (e.g., ScienceMatters).

An additional way of sharing your research with a larger audience is contributing your data to a data repository. Sharing your work on a searchable database not only extends the impact of your work but promotes new knowledge in the social sciences (Salmona et al, 2020, pp. 225–241). A growing number of data repositories around the world are available for sharing, archiving, and storing digital qualitative data. The United Kingdom Data Service (n.d.) initiative maintains an archive at the University of Essex and the United States Qualitative Data Repository (n.d.) is located at Syracuse University. For more on sharing your data, the Social Science Research Council (n.d.) has teamed with the Qualitative Data Repository (n.d.) to prepare an interactive online course, *Managing Qualitative Social Science Data*. This online course is available at no cost covering (1) planning the management of qualitative data, (2) managing qualitative data, (3) sharing qualitative data, and (4) writing with qualitative data. You are encouraged to consider these options and other similar ways to creatively share your work with others.

For more in-depth discussions on strategies to reach your audience, you may find the following resources helpful:

Belcher, W. L. (2019). *Writing your journal article in 12 weeks: A guide to academic publishing success* (2nd ed.). University of Chicago Press.

Donmoyer, R. (2012). Can qualitative researchers answer policymakers' what-works question? *Qualitative Inquiry, 18*(8), 662–673.

Hairston, M., & Keene, M. L. (2003). *Successful writing* (5th ed.). Norton.

Mewburn, I., & Clews, S. (2023). *Be visible or vanish: Engage, influence and ensure your research has impact*. Routledge. **[Part III: The Wider World]**

Renfrow, D., & Impara, J. C. (1989). Making academic presentations: Effectively! *Educational Researcher, 18*(2), 20–21.

****

As this book was inspired by the writing of Harry Wolcott, it is only fitting that we draw upon Wolcott (2009) for closing insights into the craft of qualitative writing.

I am not going to try to convince you that writing is fun. Writing is always challenging and sometimes satisfying; that is as far as I will try to go in singing its praises. You might think of it as comparable to getting up and going to work each day: Some days are more pleasant than others, but regardless of how you feel, you are expected to be "on the job," whether in an inspired state or not. (p. 5)

As the writers of this book, we attempt to do as we have written. We try and write something every day, and over time (amazingly), a substantial piece of work is created. Do not get discouraged; you now have the tools to make writing an everyday part of your personal and professional life. It may not always be enjoyable nor easy, but ultimately you will discover writing to be satisfying and rewarding. We say this as we finish this book and ponder our next adventure in writing.

REFERENCES

Anfara Jr., V. A., & Mertz, N. T. (2014). *Theoretical frameworks in qualitative research*. SAGE.

Badley, G. F. (2020). Why and how academics write. *Qualitative Inquiry*, 26(3/4), 247–256. https://doi.org/10.1177/1077800418810722

Bazeley, P. (2020). *Qualitative data analysis: Practical strategies* (2nd ed.). SAGE.

Belcher, W. L. (2019). *Writing your journal article in 12 weeks: A guide to academic publishing success* (2nd ed.). University of Chicago Press.

Biktimirov, E. N., & Nilson, L. B. (2006). Show them the money: Using mind mapping in the introductory finance course. *Journal of Financial Education*, 32(3), 72–86.

Blismas, N. G., & Dainty, A. R. J. (2003). Computer-aided qualitative data analysis: Panacea or paradox? *Building Research & Information*, 31(6), 455463.

Brodsky, A. E. (2008). In L. M. Given (Ed.), *The SAGE encyclopedia of qualitative research methods* (Vol. 2). SAGE.

Bryson, J. M. (2004). What to do when stakeholders matter, *Public Management Review*, 6(1), 21–53.

Bryson, J. M. (2018). *Strategic planning for public and nonprofit organizations: A guide to strengthening and sustaining organizational achievement* (5th ed.). Jossey-Bass.

Bryson, J. M., Patton, M., & Bowman, R. (2011). Working with evaluation stakeholders: A rationale, stepwise approach and toolkit. *Evaluation and Program Planning*, 34(1), 1–12.

Burnes, B., & Cooke, B. (2013). Kurt Lewin's field theory: A review and re-evaluation. *International Journal of Management Reviews*, 15(4), 408–425.

Burnes, B., Hughes, M., & By, R. T. (2016). Reimagining organisational change leadership. *Leadership*, 14(2), 141–158. https://doi.org/10.1177/1742715016662188

Cannella, G. S., Pérez, M. S., & Pasque, P. A. (Eds.). (2016). *Critical qualitative inquiry: Foundations and futures*. Routledge.

CAQDAS Networking Project, Department of Sociology University of Surrey Guildford Surrey, UK. (n.d.). *Computer assisted qualitative data analysis (CAQDAS) Networking Project*. https://www.surrey.ac.uk/computer-assisted-qualitative-data-analysis

Charmaz, K. (2014). *Constructing grounded theory* (2nd ed.). SAGE.

Conte, S. (n.d.). *Making a great first impression: 6 tips for writing a strong* https://www.aje.com/arc/make-great-first-impression-6-tips-writing-strong-abstract/

Coccia, M. (2018). An introduction to the theories of institutional change. *Journal of Economics Library* 5(4),

337–344. doi:10.1453/jel.v5i4.1788

Corbin, J., & Strauss, A. (2015). *Basics of qualitative research: Techniques and procedures for developing grounded theory* (4th ed.). SAGE.

Corti, L., Van den Eynden, V., Bishop, L. & Woollard, M. (2014). *Managing and sharing research data: A guide to good practice*. SAGE.

Creswell, J. W. (2009). *Research design: Qualitative, quantitative, and mixed methods approaches* (3rd ed.). SAGE.

Cummings, S., Bridgman, T., & Brown, K. G. (2016). Unfreezing change as three steps: Rethinking Kurt Lewin's legacy for change management. *Human Relations*, *69*(1), 33–60.

Davies, M. (2011). Concept mapping, mind mapping and argument mapping: What are the differences and do they matter? *Higher Education 62*(3), 279–301.

Dedoose. (2022). *Version 9.0.62, web application for managing, analyzing, and presenting qualitative and mixed method research data*. SocioCultural Research Consultants. https://www.dedoose.com

Dedoose Support Team. (2021). *Dedoose user guide: Analysis charts, tables, and plots in Dedoose*. SocioCultural Research Consultants. https://www.dedoose.com/userguide

Denzin, N. K. (1989). *Interpretive interactionism*. SAGE.

Denzin, N. K. & Lincoln, Y. S. (Ed.). (2018). *The SAGE handbook of qualitative research* (5th ed.). SAGE.

deRoche, C., & deRoche, J. E. (2010). Front stage and back stage. In A. J. Mills, G. Durepos, & E. Wiebe (Eds.), *Encyclopedia of case study research* (pp. 408–409). SAGE. http://dx.doi.org/10.4135/9781412957397.n151

Desai, V., Potter, R. B., & Potter, R. (2006). *Doing development research*. SAGE.

Dexter, C. (writer) & Bennett, E. (director). (1988). Last seen wearing (TV series episode 5). In T. Childs & K. McBain (Producers), *Inspector Morse*. Zenith Entertainment.

Donaldson M. S., Mohr J. J., Institute of Medicine (US). (2001). Exploring innovation and quality improvement in health care micro-systems: A cross-case analysis. National Academies Press. APPENDIX A, Example of Thin and Thick Description for Qualitative Analysis. https://www.ncbi.nlm.nih.gov/books/NBK223359/

Donmoyer, R. (2012). Can qualitative researchers answer policymakers' what-works question? *Qualitative Inquiry*, *18*(8), 662–673.

Dunne, C. (2011). The place of the literature review in grounded theory research. *International Journal of Social Research Methodology*, *14*(2), 111–124.

Dunne, C. & Buse, G. U. (2020). Successfully managing the literature review and write-up process when using grounded theory methodology: A dialogue in exploration. *Forum: Qualitative Social Research*, *21*(1), ISSN 1438-5627. https://www.qualitative-research.net/index.php/fqs/article/view/3338/4556

Evans, D., & Gruba, P. (2002). *How to write a better thesis* (2nd ed.). Melbourne University Press.

Farmer-Hanson, A., Gassman, J., & Shields, E. (2018). Strategic action: Community engagement professionals as institutional change leaders. *Journal of Higher Education*

Outreach and Engagement, 23(1), 197–223.

Fink, A. (2019). *Conducting research literature reviews: From the Internet to paper* (5th ed.). SAGE.

Fitzpatrick, J. L., Sanders, J. R., & Worthen, B. R. (2011). *Program evaluation: Alternative approaches and practical guidelines* (4th ed.). Allyn & Bacon.

Fossland, T., & Sandvoll, R. (2021). Drivers for educational change? Educational leaders' perceptions of academic developers as change agents. *International Journal for Academic Development*. Advance online publication. doi:10.1080/1360144X.2021.1941034

Foucault, M. (1977). *Discipline and punish: The birth of the prison*. Allen Lane.

Fullan, M. (2006). *Change theory: A force for school improvement* (Seminar Series Paper No. 157). Centre for Strategic Education.

Geertz, C. (1973). *The interpretation of cultures: Selected essays*. Basic Books.

Gibson, W., & Brown, A. (2009). *Working with qualitative data*. SAGE.

Gibson, W., & Brown, A. (2009). Theory, grounded theory and analysis. In W. Gibson & A. Brown, *Working with qualitative data* (pp. 15–32). SAGE.

Gilbert, L. S., Jackson, K., & di Gregorio S. (2014). Tools for analyzing qualitative data: The history and relevance of qualitative data analysis software. In J. Spector, M. Merrill, J. Elen, & M. Bishop (Eds.), *Handbook of research on educational communications and technology* (pp. 221–236). Springer. https://doi.org/10.1007/978-1-4614-3185-5_18

Gobby, B., & Niesche, R. (2019). Community empowerment? School autonomy, school boards and depoliticising governance. *Australian Educational Researcher, 46*(3), 565–582.

Google Images. (n.d.). from https://www.google.com/imghp

Grummert, S. E. (2021). *Carcerality and college athletics: State methods of enclosure within and through college sport* (Doctoral dissertation, University of California Riverside). https://escholarship.org/uc/item/52z8679n

Grummert, S. E. (2023). *Reflections on my findings section: Presenting participant quotes*. Unpublished manuscript.

Grunefeld, H., Prins, F. J., van Tartwijk, J., & Wubbels, T. (2021). Development of educational leaders' adaptive expertise in a professional development programme. *International Journal for Academic Development, 27*(1), 58–70. doi:10.1080/1360144X.2021.1898966

Hairston, M., & Keene, M. L. (2003). *Successful writing* (5th ed.). Norton.

Harvey, T. R. (1995). *Checklist for change: A pragmatic approach to creating and controlling change*. Technomic.

Higginbottom, G. (2015). Drawing conclusions from your research. In G. Higginbottom & P. Liamputtong (Eds.), *Participatory qualitative research methodologies in health* (pp. 80–89). SAGE. https://www.doi.org/10.4135/9781473919945

Hirschheim R., Murungi, D. M., & Pena, S. (2012). Witty invention or dubious fad? Using argument mapping to examine the contours of management fashion. *Information and Organization, 22*(1), 60–84.

Hooper, L., (n.d.). *Methodspace: Using visuals to support your writing* https://www.methodspace.co

m/using-visuals-support-writing-process/

Hughes, S. A., & Pennington, J. L. (2017). *Autoethnography: Process, product and possibility for critical social research.* SAGE.

Jacobs, R. L. (2011). Developing a research problem and purpose statement. In T. S. Rocco & T. Hatcher (Eds.), *The handbook of scholarly writing and publishing* (pp. 125–141). Jossey-Bass.

Johnson, J. L., Adkins, D., & Chauvin, S. (2020). A review of the quality indicators of rigor in qualitative research. *American Journal of Pharmaceutical Education, 81*(4), Article 7120.

Jonsen, K., Fendt, J., & Point, S. (2018). Convincing qualitative research: What constitutes persuasive writing? *Organizational Research Methods, 21*(1), 30–67.

Kaczynski, D., & Salmona, M. (2023, April 15). *Educational leadership and the forces of change: A framework for promoting community engagement.* Online Paper Repository. Annual meeting of the American Educational Research Association, Chicago, IL.

Kaczynski, D., Salmona, M., & Smith, T. (2014). Qualitative research in finance. *Australian Journal of Management, 39*(1), 127–135.

Kaefer, F., & Kaefer, P. (2020). *Introduction to Python programming for business and social science applications.* SAGE.

Kalu, M., & Norman, K. (2018). Step by step process from logic model to case study method as an approach to educational programme evaluation. *Global Journal of Educational Research, 17*(1), 73–85.

Kamler, B., & Thomson, P. (2006). *Helping doctoral students write: Pedagogies for supervision.* New York, NY: Routledge.

Kellogg Foundation, W. K. (2017). *The step-by-step guide to evaluation: How to become savvy evaluation consumers.* htttps://www.wkkf.org/

Knight, J., & Sened, I. (Eds.). (2001). *Explaining social institutions.* The University of Michigan Press.

Knowlton, L. W., & Phillips, C. C. (2013). *The logic model guidebook: Better strategies for great results* (2nd ed.). SAGE.

LeCompte, M. D. (2000). Analyzing qualitative data. *Theory into Practice, 39*(3), 146–154.

Lewin, K. (1947). Frontiers in group dynamics: Concept, method and reality in social science; equilibrium and social change. *Human Relations 1*(1), 5–41.

Lieber, E. (2016). *Harnessing discovery: Writing a strong mixed-methods proposal.* William T. Grant Foundation. https://wtgrantfoundation.org/resource/harnessing-discovery-writing-strong-mixed-methods-proposal

Lieber, E., Chin, D., Nihira, K., & Mink, I. T. (2001). Holding on and letting go: Identity and acculturation among Chinese immigrants. *Cultural Diversity and Ethnic Minority Psychology, 7*(3), 247–261. doi:10.1037/1099-9809.7.3.247

Lincoln, Y. S., & Guba, E. G. (1985). *Naturalistic inquiry.* SAGE.

Machi, L. A., & McEvoy, B. T. (2016). *The literature review: Six steps to success* (3rd ed.). SAGE.

Martelo, M. L. (2011). Use of bibliographic systems and concept maps: Innovative tools to complete a literature review. *Research in the Schools, 18*(1), 62–70.

Matias, C. E., Walker, D., & del Hierro, M. (2019). Tales from the ivory tower: Women of color's resistance to whiteness in academia. *Taboo, 18*(1), 35–58.

Marshall, C., Rossman, G. B., & Blanco, G. L. (2021). *Designing qualitative research* (7th ed.). SAGE.

Maxwell, J. A. (2013). *Qualitative research design: An interactive approach* (3rd ed.). SAGE.

Mewburn, I., & Clews, S. (2023). *Be visible or vanish: Engage, influence and ensure your research has impact.* Routledge.

Mitchell, R., Agle, B., & Wood, D. (1997). Toward a theory of stakeholder identification and salience: Defining the principle of who and what really counts. *The Academy of Management Review, 22*(4), 853–886.

MonkeyLearn. (n.d.). https://monkeylearn.com/

Nauheimer, H. (1997). *The change management toolbook. A collection of tools, methods and strategies.* https://www.change-management-toolbook.com/

Nishadha. (2021). *Creately: Using graphic organizers for writing essays, summaries and research.* https://creately.com/blog/diagrams/graphic-organizers-for-writing/

Novak, J. D., & Canas, A. J. (2008). *The theory underlying concept maps and how to construct and use them* (Technical Report IHMC Cmap Tools 2006-01 Rev 01-2008). Florida Institute for Human and Machine Cognition.

Oliver, M. (2008). *Red bird.* Beacon Press.

Olson, J. F. (1997). *Writing skills for college students.* Prentice Hall.

Ondrusek, A. L. (2012). What the research reveals about graduate students' writing skills: A literature review. *Journal of Education for Library and Information Science, 53*(3), 176–188.

O'Reilly, M., & Kiyimba, N. (2015). *Advanced qualitative research: A guide to using theory.* SAGE.

Patel, L., (2016). *Decolonizing educational research: From ownership to answerability.* Milton Routledge.

Patton, M. Q. (2015). *Qualitative research & evaluation methods* (4th ed.). SAGE.

Paulus, T., Lester, J., & Dempster, P. (2013). *Digital tools for qualitative research.* SAGE.

Piantanida, M., & Garman, N. B. (2012). *The qualitative dissertation:*

A guide for students and faculty (2nd ed.). SAGE.

Ponterotto, J. G. (2006). Brief note on the origins, evolution and meaning of the qualitative research concept "thick description." *The Qualitative Report, 11*(3), 538–549.

Purdue Online Writing Lab. (n.d.). *Prewriting.* Purdue Online Writing Lab https://owl.purdue.edu/

Pratt, M. G., Kaplan, S., & Whittington, R. (2019). Editorial Essay: The tumult over transparency: Decoupling transparency from replication in establishing trustworthy qualitative research. *Administrative Science Quarterly, 65*(1), 1–19.

Qualitative Data Repository, Center for Qualitative and Multi-Method Inquiry, a unit of the Maxwell School of Citizenship and Public Affairs at Syracuse University. (n.d.). https://qdr.syr.edu/

Renfrow, D., & Impara, J. C. (1989). Making academic presentations: Effectively! *Educational Researcher, 18*(2), 20–21.

Richards, L. (2015). *Handling qualitative data: A practical guide* (3rd ed.). SAGE.

Richards, L. (2021). *Handling qualitative data: A*

practical guide. (4th ed.). SAGE.

Rowling, J. K. (2003). Harry Potter and the Order of the Phoenix. Raincoast Books.

Saldana, J. (2013). The coding manual for qualitative researchers (2nd ed.). SAGE.

Salmona, M., Lieber, E., & Kaczynski, D. (2020). Qualitative and mixed methods data analysis using Dedoose: A practical approach for research across the social sciences. SAGE.

Salmona, M., & Kaczynski, D. (2016). Don't blame the software: Using qualitative data analysis software successfully in doctoral research. Forum Qualitative Sozialforschung / Forum: Qualitative Social Research, 17(3), Article 11. http://nbn-resolving.de/urn:nbn:de:0114-fqs1603117

Schein, E. H. (1999). Kurt Lewin's change theory in the field and in the classroom: Notes towards a model of managed learning. Reflections, 1(1), 59–74.

Schram, T. H. (2006). Conceptualizing and proposing qualitative research (2nd ed.). Merrill Prentice Hall.

Scrivener. (n.d.). The Scrivener App. https://scrivener.app/

Shank, G. (2002). Qualitative research: A personal skills approach. Merrill Prentice Hall.

Schwandt, T. A. (2015). Dictionary of qualitative inquiry (4th ed.). SAGE.

Social Science Research Council. (n.d.). Managing qualitative social science data: An interactive online course. https://managing-qualitative-data.org/

Solorzano, D. G., & Yosso, T. J. (2001). Critical race and LatCrit theory and method: Counter-storytelling. International Journal of Qualitative Studies in Education, 14(4), 471–495.

SpringerLink Publishers. (n.d.). Writing a manuscript: Titles, Abstracts & Keywords. https://www.springernature.com/gp/authors/campaigns/writing-a-manuscript/titles-abstracts-keywords

Stake, R. E. (2010). Qualitative research: Studying how things work.: Guilford Press.

Strunk Jr., W., & White, E. B. (2000). The elements of style, (4th ed.). Allyn and Bacon. https://archive.org/details/pdfy-2_qp8jQ61O16NHwa/page/n21/mode/2up

Sulphey, M. M., & Jasim, K. M. (2022). Paradoxical leadership as a moderating factor in the relationship between organizational silence and employee voice: An examination using SEM. Leadership & Organization Development Journal, 43(3), 457–481. https://doi.org/10.1108/LODJ-02-2021-0075

United Kingdom Data Service, UK Data Archive at the University of Essex. (n.d.). https://ukdataservice.ac.uk/

Wells, S. (2006). Force field analysis. Mini-Tutorial Quality Management, 15, 1–4. https://mspguide.org/2022/03/18/force-field-analysis/

Wemigwase, S., & Tuck, E. (2019). Research before and after the academy: Learning participatory Indigenous methods. In S. Windchief & T. Sa Pedro (Eds.), Applying Indigenous research methods (pp. 76–85). Routledge.

Whitty, C. (2019, January 1). How to disseminate your research. National Institute for Health Research. https://www.nihr.ac.uk/documents/how-to-disseminate-your-research/19951

Williams, J. M., & Bizup, J. (2021). Style: The basics of clarity and grace, (13th ed.). Pearson Education.

Wilson, J., Mandich, A., & Magalhães, L. (2016). Concept mapping: A

References

dynamic, individualized and qualitative method for eliciting meaning. *Qualitative Health Research, 26*(8), 1151–1161.

Wolcott, H. F. (2001a). *The art of fieldwork*. AltaMira Press.

Wolcott, H. F. (2001b). *Writing up qualitative research* (2nd ed.). SAGE.

Wolcott, H. F. (2009). *Writing up qualitative research* (3rd ed.). SAGE.

WordNet, Princeton University. (2010). *About WordNet*. https://wordnet.princeton.edu/

Writing Center, University of North Carolina at Chapel Hill. (n.d.). *Figures and charts*. https://writingcenter.unc.edu/tips-and-tools/figures-and-charts/

Youngblood Jackson, A., & Mazzei, L. (2011). *Thinking with theory in qualitative research: Viewing data across multiple perspectives*. Routledge.

Zinsser, W. (2016). *On writing well: The classic guide to writing nonfiction*, (30th ed.). HarperCollins.

Zuber-Skerritt, O. (2015). Participatory action learning and action research (PALAR) for community engagement: A theoretical framework. *Educational Research for Social Change, 4*(1), 5–25.

Zuberi, T., & Bonilla-Silva, E. (Eds.). (2008). *White logic, white methods: Racism and methodology*. Rowman & Littlefield.

INDEX

Abstract, 22, 107, 111
Advanced Image Search option, 39
Advanced writing skills, core competencies for, 13 (table)
Analytic memos, 8, 80
Argument maps, 43–44, 43 (table)
ATLAS.ti, 41
Audience
 engaging, 17–18
 identifying, 18 (table)
 story sharing, 112–114

Badley, G. F., 12
Bazeley, P., 91
Belcher, W. L., 114
Bishop, L., 77
Blismas, N. G., 79
Bookends, 41
Brainstorming, 39
Brodsky, A. E., 7
Brown, A., 92
Bryson, J. M., 52

Canas, A. J., 40
Cannella, G. S., 91
Change statement, 51
Chin, D, 111
Clews, S., 114
CMS, 41
Community engagement, 48–54, 51
Complex meanings, 86–87

Complicated sentences, 13
Composing
 conclusions, 100–102
 recommendations, 100–102
Computer Assisted Qualitative Data Analysis Networking Project (CAQDAS Networking Project), 79
ConceptDraw Diagram, 46
Concept maps, 39–40, 40 (table), 53 (figure)
Conclusions, 97–106
Confirmability, 100
Convoluted sentences, 16
Corkboard outline, 31 (figure)
Corkboard outlining, 30
Corti, L., 77
Credibility, 100, 103–106
Curriculum development, 29

Dainty, A. R. J., 79
Data
 analysis, 87–89, 88 (figure)
 analysis and interpretation, 90–92, 90 (table)–91 (table)
 connections, 69

definition, 70–71
digital tools, 73–75, 77–78
Google Forms, 75–76, 75 (figure)–76 (figure)
interviews, 72 (table)
management, 77–80, 78–80
organizing, 71–73
relationships in, 89–90
sorting, 71–73
storage for, 77 (table)
thick description, 80–83
types of, 72 (table)
Data-tracking system, 78
Davies, M., 43
Dedoose, 41
Delivering value, 97–98
Denzin, N. K., 81–82, 92
Dependability, 100
Desai, V., 42
Diagrams, 19
Digital tools, 21–22, 21 (table), 25, 74–75
Digital writing
 definition, 20–21
 records, 73
Distilling emergent meanings, 85–86
Document framework, 23–30
Donmoyer, R., 114

Edraw Max, 46
Educational leadership, 29, 48–54

123

Educational reform, 29
Endnote, 35, 41

Findings from meanings
　complex meanings,
　　86-87
　developing connections during
　　analysis, 87-89
　distilling emergent
　　meanings,
　　85-86
　researcher's reflections on, 92-95
Focus statement, 6-7
Force-field analysis,
　51, 52
Forces of change, 48-54
Framing, 23-30

Gibson, W., 92
Gliffy, 46
Google Docs, 22, 73
Google Forms, 73, 75
　data export for, 76
　(table)
Google Images, 39,
　45-46
GPS devices, 73
Grummert, Sara E.,
　92-95

Hairston, M., 114
Heading styles, 25-27
Head off momentum-killing procrastination, 11-12
Hirschheim R., 44
HTML text, 72

Impara, J. C., 114
Inductive-deductive
　shifts memos,
　8-9
Institutional Capacity, 51

Institutional stakeholders, 51
Instrument, researcher as, 4-5

Kaczynski, D., 111
Kalu, M., 44
Keene, M. L., 114
Killing procrastination,
　11-12
Knowlton, L. W., 44

Language, 86
LeCompte, M. D., 92
Lieber, E., 111
Lincoln, Y. S., 92
Literature maps, 40-42,
　41 (table), 54
　(figure)
Literature, referencing,
　102-103
Logic models, 44, 44
　(table)
Lucidchart, 46

Machi, L. A., 42
Magalhães, L., 40
Mandich, A., 40
Martelo, M. L., 40
MAXQDA, 41
Maxwell, J. A., 7, 92
McEvoy, B. T., 42
Memos, 19
Mendeley, 41
Methods memos, 8
Mewburn, I., 114
Microsoft Power Point,
　46
Microsoft Vizio, 46
Microsoft Word, 23,
　25-26, 46
Mind maps, 42-43,
　42 (table), 50
　(figure)
Mink, I. T., 111
Momentum, 9-12

head off momentum-killing procrastination, 11-12
　strategies, 9, 10 (table)
　switch modes to,
　10-11
Murungi, D. M., 44

Naming convention,
　33-35
Navigation pane, 26
Nihira, K., 111
Norman, K., 44
Novak, J. D., 40
NVivo, 41

Organizational change
　theory, 29,
　48-54
Organizational positioning, 51
Organizing
　capture ideas, free
　writing to,
　30-32
　frame, 25-30
　planning, 23-25
　saving everything,
　32-35
　structuring, 25-32

Papers, 41
Pasque, P. A., 91
Patton, M. Q., 7
PDF, 41, 73
Pena, S., 44
Pérez, M. S., 91
Phillips, C. C., 44
Ponterotto, J. G., 119
Potter, R. B., 42
Princeton University, 39
Process, 2-3, 3 (table)-4
　(table), 12-14
Procrastination opportunities, 11
　(figure)

Professional teaching practices, 29
Project writing targets, 32 (figure)
Publication, 108–112
Purpose statement, 6–7

Qualitative conclusions, 98–100
Qualitative data analysis software program (QDAS), 41
Qualitative memos, 7–9, 8 (table)
Qualitative research, 17
Quality indicators, credibility, 103–106
Qualtrics, 75

README file, 72, 78
Recommendations, 97–106
References, keeping track of, 35
Reflective memos, 8
RefWorks, 41
Renfrow, D., 114
Research
   audience, 17–18, 18 (table)
   design, 18–19
   digital, 20–22, 21 (table)
   gather and use, 19–20
   story articulating, 16–17
   trail building, 19
Research design
   argument, 62–65
   linking to theory, 59–60
   research focus, 60–61
   research questions, 60–61
   voices in, 65–68
Research focus, 60–61
   strategies to, 61–62

Research maps
   argument maps, 43–44, 43 (table)
   concept maps, 39–40, 40 (table), 53 (figure)
   literature maps, 40–42, 41 (table), 54 (figure)
   logic models, 44, 44 (table)
   making, 39
   mind maps, 42–43, 42 (table), 50 (figure)
Research questions, 4, 6, 19–20, 57, 60–62
Revision strategies, 107–108
Richards, L., 73, 92

Salmona, M., 7, 111
Saving everything
   naming convention, 33–35
   references, keeping track of, 35
   version control, 32–33, 34 (table)
Schram, T. H., 92
Schwandt, T. A., 81
Scrivener, 22, 30–31
Shank, G., 81
SmartDraw, 46
Spreadsheets, 19
Stakeholder analysis, 51, 52
Stake, R. E., 40
Stilted language, 16
Story sharing
   larger audience, 112–114
   publication, 108–112
   revision strategies, 107–108
Strategic management processes, 52

Styles, 25–26
SurveyGizmo, 75
SurveyMonkey, 75

Table of contents (ToC), 27–28
Title, qualities of, 110 (table)
Transferability, 100

Value, delivering, 97–98
Van den Eynden, V., 77
Verbal communication, 11
Version control, 32–33, 34 (table)
Virtual index cards, 30
Visualizing
   definition, 37
   example, 48–55
   research maps. *See* Research maps
   using maps to, 45–48
VisualParadigm Online, 46

Wilson, J., 40
Wolcott, H. F., 1–2, 23, 101
Woollard, M., 77
WordNet Search, 39
Writing
   advanced writing skills, core competencies for, 13 (table)
   data. *See* Data
   focus statement, 6–7
   fundamental elements in, 3 (table)–4 (table)
   instrument, researcher as, 4–5
   momentum, 9–12

organizing. *See*
Organizing
process, 2–3, 3
(table)–4 (table),
12–14
purpose statement, 6–7

qualitative memos,
7–9, 8 (table)
questions, 14 (table)
strategies, 9, 10
(table)
thinking about

visualizing. *See*
Visualizing
voices in, 65–68

Zotero, 41